PARABLE OF THE BROWN GIRL

PARABLE OF THE BROWN GIRL

THE SACRED LIVES OF GIRLS OF COLOR

fortress press

MINNEAPOLIS

PARABLE OF THE BROWN GIRL

The Sacred Lives of Girls of Color

Print ISBN: 978-1-5064-5568-6

eBook ISBN: 978-1-5064-5569-3

The names of the people included in this book have been changed to protect their identities.

Cover design: Josh Dingle, LoveArts

For all the brown-skinned black girls who courageously shared
their story, their wisdom, and their truths with me.

Society may put you on the margins,
but you are at the center of God's heart.

CONTENTS

Acknowledgments

Exactly one week after I signed the contract with Fortress Press to write this book, one of the most important people in the world to me passed away. It is only fitting I begin by acknowledging the person who was on my mind every single day for the nine months it took me to write this book.

Roy Andre Drakeford, aka "Mugga."

I didn't imagine how it would feel to write through grief, but the words for this book came to me as I was experiencing a profound loss. Somehow, I got through it. I can only believe I was able to because of God's spirit and the impeccable work ethic Mugga passed on to me. I not only acknowledge you, Mugga, for this book, but I also acknowledge you for my entire life. I was an insecure, angry, and broken fifteen-year-old black girl when we met. Your love and friendship breathed life into me. We had fun, we laughed, we cried, and you loved this black girl into wholeness. I will never forget you. I owe you my life, and I will love you always from now until eternity.

Mom and Dad, if I had only written a handful of words in this book, you both still would have put the support of ten thousand angels behind me with your unconditional love. There are no real words of gratitude I can write to thank you for my very existence, for listening to all my big ideas, for supporting those ideas, for attending every event, for financing every project, for catching me when I fall, and for loving me through every failure and mistake. I am forever indebted to you. I do not take for granted that you, like Christ, are an expression of God's love for me.

To Valerie Weaver-Zercher, Emily Brower, and Fortress Press. Thank you for taking a chance on this black girl and subsequently supporting and acknowledging the significance of all of the black girls in this book. Thank you for your gracious and constructive thoughts, affirmations, and critiques to help bring out the message and potential of this book.

Finally, to all of my friends, family, mentors, and community of supporters who have been my cheering squad before, during, and long after this book is finished. If the company we keep is a reflection of who we are, then I am proud to be a reflection of each and every one of you.

Introduction

People resist by . . . telling their story.
—bell hooks[1]

J esus Christ did some of his most valuable teaching in parables. His parables presented clear stories from everyday circumstances where the listener would be met by the spirit of God alongside plain truths. In thinking on the times in my life when I have had those same profound encounters, those moments have undoubtedly been in my interactions and conversations with black girls. Consequently, I have often wondered what these parables would have looked like with black girls at the center. *Parable of the Brown Girl* explores the everyday lives of black girls and is written in a way that parallels some of the characteristics of the parables of the gospels. For starters, the names of Jesus's parables usually emphasize an important feature of either the central character(s) of the parable or theme. In staying true to that manner, I created this book title with an emphasis on the color of the girls' skin, which many would distinctly see as brown. I specifically use the phrase *brown girl* in the book and chapter titles to highlight the variety of hues the girls have in their skin complexions. However, when referencing the girls throughout the content of the book, I refer to them as black. Racially classified, they are black; aesthetically the girls are shades of brown.

In each place my career has taken me, I have had the opportunity to develop powerful relationships with black girls. My life has been significantly impacted for the better by listening to these girls. My conversations with them have changed how I see God and how I see the world around me. The first of these experiences happened when I graduated from college. I worked briefly at a residential treatment facility where I was placed on a unit for teenaged girls suffering from severe emotional difficulties. Although I was only a twenty-one-year-old recent graduate who'd spent the previous four years of college studying advertising, the hiring process for this position as a residential counselor was effortless. However, the turnover rate for this position was at about 70 percent. I didn't understand the reasons for this high percentage until I stepped foot onto the unit for the first time and looked into the faces of nine angry black girls. They were angry with the world around them for letting them down. They were angry for being left and forgotten in this jail-like facility in a remote corner of the country, and they wanted everyone they encountered to feel that same anger.

As a staff, we were trained to meet the girls' coldness with coldness. We had strict instructions not to get into overt close relationship with the girls, though we could do so subtly. During my first month there, I worked hard to enforce the rules, maintaining strict boundaries with the girls and making sure they respected my authority. The girls didn't care about any of those things. To them, I was just another person who was there for a paycheck and who would likely leave them soon. They tested me, cursed at me, manipulated me, and disrespected me every chance they got. After a while, I began to understand why the turnover rate was so high.

One night while completing my evening notes before my shift was over, I decided to take a look through some of the girls' binders. Each had a binder full of notes written by the staff. The binders also contained background information on the girls. Each girl had her own story. I read nine-year-old Leticia had once been beaten with a baseball bat by her mom. I read ten-year-old India had been sexually abused by her own father. I read seven-year-old Nikki had been burned with cigarettes for misbehaving in the house. It was like perusing a book with pages no one would ever see. I remember feeling nauseous reading each of the horrifying stories. These girls were far more than bad kids who needed to be locked up in order to behave.

That was the first time I sensed the call God placed on my life to build relationships and work as an advocate for black girls who often find themselves on the margins. After learning their stories, everything about my entire approach to working with those nine girls changed. I spent the next few months getting to know each girl personally. I listened to them share their stories. I watched them get so angry, staff would have to physically carry them to their rooms so they would calm down. I watched them laugh with black girl joy with each other in random moments as if they'd forgotten they were locked away. I saw the pain on their faces when family would say they were coming to visit and then failed to show up at the last minute. I worked so many hours there were times I would tuck the girls in at night, go home to sleep, and then be back the next morning in time to wake them up. I stopped treating the girls like a job or like they were inmates, and the girls began to let their guards down more and more. They nicknamed me "Advocate" because that was what they called staff they trusted. They showed me pictures of their families and we stayed up at night talking about their crushes on boys and which staff they couldn't stand. Sometimes, we talked about God and prayer, and we would pray together at night before it was time for lights out.

After a little under a year, I left the residential treatment facility upon getting a new job with another youth program. I struggled with the decision, knowing I would be one more person who had come into the girls' lives just to leave them. Before my last day, I bought them all journals, Bibles, and stuffed bears. I also spent time handwriting all nine girls personal letters, telling each of them why they were special to me and why they were special to God. On that last day, I gave them their letters and gifts before leaving, and I will never forget the tears we all shed as we grieved the end of our season together. I distinctly remember telling the girls I knew I had to leave because I needed to go help other girls just like them to give voice to their own stories.

It has been fifteen years since my time at that residential treatment facility. My career has taken me into a variety of spaces, and in each one, I have had the privilege to experience a group of black girls with vivacious spirits and colorful personalities. They each have a story to tell, just like the girls at the residential treatment facility at my first job. Typically, their lives are ones of amazing resilience while being discounted and overlooked, unseen and unheard. In my career, I have combined my education and pastoral practices to address the reality of black girls' lives and experiences. I have been a teacher to black girls in educational settings. I have been a counselor to black girls in therapeutic settings. I have been a pastor to black girls in pastoral settings. I have been a mentor to black girls in community-based settings. The stories in this book come from my experiences with black girls in each of those varied environments.

Through these experiences, I often imagine how any number of the girls I meet could find themselves in one of Jesus's parables, the stories he used to illustrate a moral or spiritual lesson. He frequently focused his parables on the neglected and unnoticed, highlighting wisdom and strength where they had previously been ignored. These girls, too, are neglected and unnoticed. They are also wise and full of incredible strength. As Monique Morris writes, "The way forward is to listen to and incorporate the voices and experiences of young women who have been overlooked in the current discourse."[2] *Parable of the*

Brown Girl builds the way forward by celebrating the voices and experiences of black girls who have gone unseen for too long.

The similarities of these girls' struggles amaze me. Oftentimes when I would hear one girl share her story, I couldn't help but think about another girl with very comparable struggles and circumstances. These are not only similarities with each other's stories, but also similarities with black women's stories across generations. I recognize their struggles and experiences in my own life. As I walked through the Smithsonian National Museum of African American History and Culture and read about the lives of other black women and girls dating back to the 1500s, the cultural challenges those women faced then were very much like the ones contemporary young black women had now. Their stories shared profound spiritual wisdom while highlighting the grave cultural truths about how society viewed and treated black women, which both were long overdue for serious revolutionary change.

I hope readers will encounter the spirit of God within these girls' stories just like they do through Jesus's parables, which encouraged others to reflect on spiritual truths through the lives of the overlooked. In their stories, the girls reflect on their circumstances, asking tough questions and finding ways to draw wisdom so they can make sense of God and the world around them. Their musings give insight into how God works through the minds of these young black girls, and every story demonstrates how God's spirit works through each girl to convey a specific message. I hope the truth and wisdom found here changes how people treat each other. These girls' stories are important to God—these *girls* are important to God—and they deserve attention.

These girls have been left to navigate adolescence and fight against systemic inequalities on their own, leaving their stories overlooked, ignored, and on the margins of the public discourse. Yet this book centers their experiences so their circumstances can resonate with people, no matter their ethnicity, race, faith, or background. Everyone will learn something from these girls' stories, questions, and conclusions. As Christie Cozad Neuger says, "Parables are about people having their ordinary lives respected and valued as a way to experience God."[3] I intend to prioritize these girls and their experiences so everyone will begin to respect and value their existence, and to experience God in a richer, more beautiful way.

Parable of the
WEAK BROWN GIRL

Why would God make me a warrior when I'm really just weak?
—Deborah, age nine

For a nine-year-old girl, Deborah had a very sharp and opinionated mind. She was curious and perceptive, yet also quite innocent.

About a week prior to Deborah's ninth birthday, her mother brought her to see me for counseling. She wanted Deborah to have someone to share her inquisitive thoughts with outside of her family and friends. In the time we'd been seeing one another, Deborah and I talked about many things. She often described school as her "happy place." One could feel the warmth of her big, bright smile when she talked about her friends and her classes. At school she felt safe, contrary to what she described as feeling trapped at home. She lived in a small, one-bedroom apartment with her mother and her mother's boyfriend, who was recently released from jail after two years. Before he returned, Deborah slept in a room with her mother, which she loved because of how close she felt to her mother physically and emotionally.

Now she slept in the living room on their big, dusty, brown couch, which she described as old and worn. The middle dipped low when she lay on the couch and she often awoke with her back aching, but her mother thought Deborah was being dramatic when she complained about it. However, Deborah's grievances indicated she felt distance between her and her mother and no longer had a sense of security and safety at home. Deborah's mother was usually tired from working most of the day to support herself, her daughter, and her boyfriend. It had been six months since her mother's boyfriend had moved in, and Deborah didn't feel comfortable with him in her home. When she told her mother this, her words fell on deaf ears, just like all her other complaints did. Her mother thought Deborah was jealous but also believed Deborah would adjust to the situation eventually.

Searching for solutions, Deborah considered going to live with her father and his family who lived only twenty minutes away from them in a much bigger house than her tiny apartment. His townhouse was in a quaint, middle-class suburban neighborhood, a huge contrast from Deborah's low-income and crime-ridden one. Her father and mother had never married and Deborah had never lived with her father, so she'd always felt like he didn't want her. He even had a family of his own now with a wife, a stepdaughter around Deborah's age, and a baby on the way. Deborah wanted to live with them because their lives seemed simpler, more stable, and peaceful. Yet, every time she visited them, she felt unwelcome. While there, she shared a room with a stepsister who didn't like her. And while Deborah was grateful to have her own twin bed to sleep in, she still felt uncomfortable because of her stepsister's coldness. Deborah also thought her stepmother ignored her and her father maintained his distance because he didn't want to upset his new family.

"It's 'cause they don't like me," Deborah reasoned.

One evening, Deborah's mother went out with her boyfriend without leaving dinner for her. Hungry and frustrated, Deborah had had enough. She mustered up the courage to ask her father if she could move in with him.

"Daddy," she cried into the phone.

"What's wrong honey?" he responded.

"I want to come live with you!"

After a short pause, he said he would call her back. After waiting by the phone, she eventually fell asleep. Waking up hours later, Deborah realized he never returned her call.

"He doesn't want me, and neither does she," she vented as we sat in one of our weekly counseling sessions. Deborah was angry, hurt, and depressed. Her challenging circumstances started affecting her schoolwork. Her teachers sent messages home, expressing concern over the change in her behavior.

"Maybe she needs to see a psychiatrist," one wrote.

Concerned, her mother brought her to see me more frequently. Deborah acknowledged having a hard time concentrating in school, but she still felt like it was the safest place for her to be.

"Do you feel like you have an advocate?" I asked.

"What's that?"

"An advocate is someone who is on your side. Someone you can turn to who understands you."

She paused, thinking for a moment. "No," she eventually responded. "No one."

Deborah had a black-and white-marbled composition notebook she used as her journal. She didn't structure her thoughts in a particular way, filling the notebook mostly with pencil-drawn pictures and poems. Knowing these were her private thoughts, I told Deborah she did not have to read them to me. Sometimes, she would bring the

3

journal and have it idly on the desk. Other times, she wanted to read her thoughts from the past week. One day as she read, I glanced into the notebook and saw a picture she'd drawn, but I couldn't quite make out who or what it was.

"What's that?" I asked.

Embarrassed, she tried to hide it, but I promised I wouldn't judge anything she drew or wrote. When she showed me the picture more closely, I was horrified. It was a picture of a girl with a gun to her head and the words "What's the point? No one cares." Something inside of me knew Deborah was the little girl. I asked her about the picture and she said it was an old drawing. Upon seeing the concerned look on my face, she tried to reassure me she'd just been having a bad day when she'd drawn it.

We sat in silence for a moment while I tried to gather words. Deborah seemed more concerned with my reaction than the actual drawing, and I sensed she didn't want me to worry. But I continued to analyze the picture. There were no colors, only the lining from the pencil. The little girl's face had big, oval-shaped eyes with cascading tears down her cheeks. The girl wore a dress and had two ponytails in her hair. When I finally found the words, I tried my hardest to impress to her that her life was important and that although things were difficult, people loved and cared for her. I also told her she had a life with purpose just like everyone else and God hadn't made a mistake when creating her. She paused to think about my words and then desperately asked one of the most profound questions I'd ever heard.

"Why did God make me a warrior when I'm really just weak?"

I'd explained to Deborah that we would journey through life's questions during our time together. I'd warned I wouldn't always have the answers, but we would do our best to find them. This was a time I had no answer. As our session for that particular day ended, I promised we would revisit her question the next time, which would be the following week. As the intervening days passed, I grappled with her question, unable to get it out of my head. I was also ashamed to admit I had been in that exact theological crisis more times than I could count. Why *did* God make *me* a warrior, when I, just like Deborah, was simply a weak human being? Numerous challenging moments in my life have led me to question my abilities. When I would outwardly struggle, people would quote, "He will not let you be tempted beyond your ability" (1 Corinthians 10:13). However, my abilities felt like failures. It was—and still is—hard to admit to feeling this weakness, even though I had been in leadership positions before where I had to portray strength. I realized a nine-year-old could articulate one of life's important questions in a way that I never could.

Nevertheless, I knew I'd have to tell Deborah something more than typical, "You're not weak—don't say that. You're brave and strong." Why did we respond with this comforting platitude even though it was not the truth for most of us? Adults especially give these types of fabrications when communicating with children, believing to protect them from painful realities. Was it better to tell a child uncomfortable truths at a young age or to lie so they can maintain unchallenged happiness? In this case, I did not want to lie. I had to tell Deborah the truth, which meant I needed to figure out an appropriate response to her question.

A week later, I went to our next session with the intention to pick up where we left off. I waited for her nervously and quietly. Deborah walked into the sparsely decorated room and sat across from me at our usual table. I couldn't tell if she looked tired because of a long day at school or because of her sleepless nights on her couch at home. I told her I had been thinking about her question all week and I finally had an answer. As I looked into the face of that troubled yet innocent

5

nine-year-old little girl, I said, "Just because you are weak, doesn't make you less than a warrior. Warriors can be weak." She might not have grasped the totality of that statement, but nevertheless, she looked relieved to know she could still be considered a warrior. Her weakness did not negate her strength.

If our truest selves are not always strong, why do we place such emphasis and privilege on constantly embodying strength? This quandary is a theological and human in nature, and one many black women and girls especially have to face throughout their lives.

> *We're told to be tough, but life can*
> *wear down even the most resilient of us.*
> —Whit Taylor

I experienced an emotionally challenging season when I couldn't leave my bed for a month, replaying events repeatedly in my mind and wondering what I could have done differently, where had I taken the wrong turn. Impulsively, I shut my cell phone off for a few weeks and then changed my number when I finally decided to turn it back on. I isolated myself from some of the people closest to me and spent a great deal of time binge-watching Netflix and taking long walks with my dog. Once I started feeling better, I emerged slowly and attended social gatherings and church more frequently.

In the aftermath, I had a conversation with someone I admired. He asked me where had I been, and because I trusted him I said I'd been depressed for the past month and was still in recovery. I never forgot his response.

"You are too talented, too gifted, and have too much strength to be depressed."

I nervously laughed it off and we moved on to the next subject. I'd expected more compassion. Though his reply might sound like a compliment on the surface, it was actually unhelpful and discouraging. After we parted ways, questions flooded my mind: What did my talents have to do with my inability to handle the pressures of life? What did my gifts have to do with my emotional state? Why was I only given space to be strong?

This isn't the first time someone wanted a superhuman display of emotional strength in the face of my despair. I'm constantly told that as a black woman, especially a confident and self-reliant one, I should be able to handle even the most challenging circumstances with ease. I'm told I must manage my emotions with more grace. I have no space to be human.

My conversation with Deborah made me reflect on everyone's expectations for me to be strong all the time and how they had affected my own life. I realized I didn't have much—if any—permission to be weak. The message was always black women were strong; therefore I had to be, no matter what.

THE STRONG BLACK WOMAN

Contessa Louise Cooper sought therapy after experiencing a failed marriage, several miscarriages, and having full responsibility for caring for an autistic son. However, the damaging advice she received led her to write "An Open Letter to My Therapist Who Called Me A 'Strong Black Woman,'"[4]

> I told you about me, my struggles, and how I was feeling inside. You sat there in your expensive clothing, your perfectly decorated office, and smiled at me the entire time. When I finished being open, vulnerable, and raw, you said words that would haunt me to this day. "You seem like a STRONG BLACK WOMAN, and found ways to cope. I'm proud of you. Please come back if you feel like life is too much to handle." Why didn't you hear me? Why didn't you acknowledge the internal battle between me, my culture, and my faith that I

had to overcome? Why didn't you see all of me? Why did you ignore the tears that streamed down my cheeks? Why didn't you know that I had had enough of being "strong?"

The archetype of the strong black woman originated during slavery, created to validate the abuses black women endured and the resiliency they exhibited as a result. The strong black woman stereotype normalizes constant strife, stress, and challenges as natural parts of a young black girl's life that she must endure with superhuman independence and emotional containment. Trudier Harris writes,

> These superhuman female characters have been denied the "luxuries" of failure, nervous breakdowns, leisured existences, or anything else that would suggest they are complex, multidimensional characters. They must swallow their pain, gird their loins against trouble . . . and persist in spite of adversity.[5]

The thought that black women possess a certain level of power confers honor and distinction, but it also sacrifices their ability to be vulnerable, leaving no room for weakness. As a result, the strong black woman stereotype works against many girls and women rather than for them. Yes, Deborah *is* strong. She has a unique strength and recognizes herself as a warrior even as a nine-year-old child. However, she sees weakness as a liability instead of as part of who she is as a child of God. Deborah thinks for her life to have any value, she must maintain her warrior strength at all times. Because of this, she sees her warrior image as a curse and herself as a failure.

On the one hand, we must teach young black girls to be warriors who are capable of doing whatever they set their minds on. They need to know they have the strength within them to conquer whatever obstacles lie ahead. On the other hand, we must allow these girls to have moments of vulnerability instead of having to be self-reliant at all times because no one will be there to rescue them. They must experience being the recipients of caring and understanding.

I once sat in a feminist studies lecture where the professor showed a video of how women are typically portrayed in media, particularly in films. We watched illustrations of princesses and princes rescuing damsels in distress. The lecture presented these images as problematic because the consistent message within these films was women needed rescuing. However, the professor didn't acknowledge these were mostly white women being rescued, an often-ignored dynamic in many feminist circles. What effect did watching these types of films have on black girls? What effect did it have on *me*? I didn't look like Ariel, Belle, or even Princess Jasmine, despite her slightly darker skin complexion compared to the others. I didn't even look like the supporting characters. While many of my white girlfriends certainly saw themselves in these films, daydreaming about their own happy endings and dressing up as those Disney princesses on Halloween, I never saw myself in any of those princesses, and not just because they weren't black. Even though I loved watching the films growing up, I realized much later that my experience watching these films was quite different from my white friends'.

I asked a group of black girls what messages they received when watching typical animated fairy-tale films.

> I watched all the Disney princess movies because they were my favorite growing up. I pretty much watched them on repeat. But I didn't think I could be a Disney princess. They didn't look like me or act like me. I hated my hair and my skin. I had a little more sass than them too. —Sixteen years old

> I grew up around a lot of black women in my family. They always told me, "Remember you can rescue yourself." Girls like me didn't get rescued so I think they were trying to prepare me. —Fourteen years old

9

Princess Jasmine still looked Western as hell. She's like a white person with a tan. I was offended by Jasmine the most because she was the token minority for Disney. —Sixteen years old

I thought they were cool, but it never occurred to me that they should resonate [with] me as a child. It was something separate. The films were so otherworldly. There was no way that could be me so I looked at it from the inside out. I watched my white friends dress up as these princesses, but I knew that it wasn't for me. —Fifteen years old

This need to be strong starts burdening girls at a young age and ultimately leaves them under-protected and undervalued. No one will rescue them; they must rescue themselves. Black girls rarely cry out for help because when they do, no one answers.

While the overall feminist message for girls reasserts and emphasizes strength and confidence in general, we have to acknowledge that there is a conflicting dynamic that exists for young black girls. The positive feminist message proves counteractive and blind to the plight of black girls. What is known as feminist power for white girls gets characterized as aggression in black girls. What is known as feminist empowerment for white women reduces black girls to being angry. Even in the most unintentional ways, imbalanced messaging perpetuates these stereotypes. A study from the Georgetown Law Center on Poverty and Inequality titled *Girl Interrupted: The Erasure of Black Girls' Childhood*[6] found, compared to white girls of the same age, survey participants think:

- Black girls need less nurturing
- Black girls need less protection
- Black girls need to be supported less
- Black girls need to be comforted less
- Black girls are more independent

Perceptions like these findings present the innate strength of black women and girls as permission for the world to offer them less care or to see them as too aggressive. A parent of a ten-year-old I mentor forwarded me an email from one of her daughter's teachers. Her daughter was in trouble for not being prepared in class and for excessive talking. The teacher threatened to give her daughter detention and, according to the teacher, the girl wasn't upset. In an email to the girl's mother, the teacher wrote, "I will hold back on her consequences. I'm actually not going to rush with this issue. What I am noticing is that nothing phases her. It's puzzling to me how strong her personality seems to be."

The email made me angry. The teacher didn't see the girl as a typical ten-year-old student pretending not to care about getting in trouble in school, but rather as a child who let the bad things that happen to her roll off her back. *Girl Interrupted* highlighted a study by Professor Edward W. Morris where teachers described young black girls as "exhibiting 'very "mature" behavior, socially (but not academically) sophisticated, and "controlling at a young age." ' This interpretation of black girls' outspokenness may be associated with the stereotype of black women as aggressive and dominating."[7] Instead of ascribing a positive value to the girl's self-possessed personality, the teacher invalidated it as a negative trait. The girl's strength became a weakness and a failure.

The strong black woman archetype puts black women in a lose-lose situation. In order to endure challenges with minimal support they receive, black women's very strength gets labeled as aggression. In her article "Maxine Waters and the Burden of the 'Strong Black Woman,'" Vanessa Williams writes, "the overexposed image of the strong black woman also puts African American girls and women at risk for violence and harsher treatment by society."[8]

With this overexposure comes the belief that black women and girls can handle anything, including things beyond any reasonable expectation of the strength one person can sustain. I sat with a sixteen-year-old black girl and asked how she felt about the strong black woman narrative:

> There is no way a black woman can be vulnerable. People always think that we have to carry everything. It's like that Zora Neale Hurston book *Their Eyes Were Watching God*. The black woman is the mule. Everything goes on her back and people think that she can tough it out. I don't know if you've seen Childish Gambino's video of Michelle Obama hugging Kanye West, but when I saw it I was thinking that black women don't need to cut themselves on the broken pieces of messed-up black men. No, I refuse to do that. It's time that we stop seeing women of color as something that everyone owns or that we have to carry everyone.

In 1966, musician and civil rights activist Nina Simone wrote the song "Four Women," highlighting four archetypes of black women. The first woman in the song, Aunt Sarah, sings, "My back is strong. Strong enough to take the pain inflicted again and again."[9] Aunt Sarah represents the extraordinary strength in the face of constant pain many of her gender and race must endure. After Nina Simone died in 2003, Thulani Davis wrote a piece in homage to Simone, saying "[Four Women] acknowledged the loss of childhoods among African American women, our invisibility, exploitation, defiance, and even subtly reminded that in slavery and patriarchy, your name is what *they* call you."[10] This burden of strength black women carry renders their pain invisible, tasking these women to endure this unseen pain all alone for the rest of their lives without remedy.

The strong black woman archetype is a heavy mantle for a little girl to carry. As a result, there are not many spaces where black girls can be vulnerable, innocent, and supported.

I made it my responsibility to see Deborah in the ways Contessa Louis Cooper's therapist failed to do. I had to reverse the narrative. I'm not sure if Deborah knew she was inhabiting the strong black woman archetype, but I knew she felt she had no option but to be strong. I had to offer her a new narrative most young black girls didn't get to hear: she could express all parts of her story—the warrior and the damsel.

> Each time he said, "My grace is all you need. My power works best in weakness." So now I am glad to boast about my weaknesses, so that the power of Christ can work through me. That's why I take pleasure in my weaknesses, and in the insults, hardships, persecutions, and troubles that I suffer for Christ. For when I am weak, then I am strong.
>
> —2 Corinthians 12:9–10 NLT

WHY DID GOD MAKE HER A WARRIOR?

Deborah and I were in a theological and existential crisis. With weakness as her constant reality, Deborah questioned her purpose as a warrior.

"What makes a person a warrior?" I asked.

She responded with words like "fearless," "strong," and "hero."

I then asked, "What makes a person weak?"

According to Deborah, weak people were cowards—emotional and helpless. In her mind, real warriors should never experience any of these vulnerable feelings. Deborah acknowledged the tension between weakness and strength but assumed she had to be one or the other. She knew God created her to be a warrior, but she felt her weaknesses negated her calling. I knew she didn't think there was a place for her weakness with God.

Deborah's question highlighted a critical theological paradox facing all human beings: the spiritual juxtaposition of strength and weakness. We have done a great disservice to ourselves by polarizing weakness and strength when it comes to how we talk about the human experience. We separate them into groups, as though one has to be at odds with the other, when it is the tension between the two that makes us human. Theologically speaking, there are many biblical examples one can look to regarding strength and weakness. To me, the most significant example is Jesus Christ. Jesus is the exemplary model of power, strength, and weakness coexisting in one person. Jesus was both powerful as God and weak as a human being.

In 1 Corinthians 1:27, God chose the weak things of the world to shame the strong. Jesus exemplified this passage with his weak disposition—antithetical to cultural expectations for a man who was supposed to be both King and Messiah. The people of Israel believed God would continue God's pattern of redeeming them by sending a mighty king who fought battles and ruled through power. Israel had an entire history of living within cycles of turmoil and triumph, exclusion and community, exile and captivity. With those cycles came messages of hope: "'I will send my messenger, who will prepare the way before me. Then suddenly the Lord you are seeking will come to his temple; the messenger of the covenant, whom you desire, will come,' says the Lord Almighty" (Malachi 3:1).

The Israelites were looking forward to the arrival of their messiah. They dreamed of a king coming to restore the community and kingdom. They expected a powerful force whose presence would tower over all of their adversaries and eradicate evil in one heroic act of resistance. Jesus didn't quite present himself that way. Instead, he was a vulnerable human. When we read Scripture about Jesus's life now, we easily highlight the moments of power and supernatural wisdom, but we fail to acknowledge just how disenfranchised Jesus actually was. Jesus was born into poverty and on the margins of society. His family was from a small town of no real historical significance. Simply put, Jesus was born an outcast.

As Jesus's ministry progressed, he often used what we would consider backward teaching to highlight the essence of the kingdom of God. He would say things like "the last shall be first, and the first last" (Matthew 20:16). In his beatitudes in Luke, Jesus said, "God blesses you who are poor, for the Kingdom of God is yours. God blesses you who are hungry now, for you will be satisfied. God blesses you who weep now, for in due time you will laugh" (Luke 6:20–36). Contrary to our human thinking, Jesus claimed surrendering to vulnerable dispositions was the gateway to spiritual transformation. Therefore, weakness becomes a divine imperative for God to reveal his power through us.

GOD-LIKE STRENGTH OF BLACK WOMEN AND GIRLS

Black women and girls possess a strength that can only come from the Holy Spirit. At the same time, black women and girls have weaknesses just like everyone else. The strong black woman image prevents society from truly seeing black women and girls in their holiness and their humanity. This results in frustration, depletion, and, subsequently, anger. Consider Donna Kate Rushin's piece, "The Bridge Poem," as a protest against this treatment, especially with the line, "I will not be the bridge to your womanhood."[11] She is tired of having to be the bridge, of using her strength to carry the community and the world around her. Because of her strength, people turn to the black woman for remedies, answers, and other resources. She not only serves as people's passage from one point to another, but also as a platform that carries the weight of whoever wants to pass over her. Rushin's poem bears striking similarities to the image of the suffering servant in Isaiah 53:4–6 (which is often interpreted as a messianic prophecy about Jesus). Like black women, the suffering servant bears and carries the burdens of other people through his own strength.

15

Surely he has borne our griefs
And carried our sorrows;
Yet we esteemed him stricken,
Smitten by God, and afflicted.
But he was pierced for our transgressions,
He was crushed for our iniquities;
Upon him was the chastisement that brought us peace,
And with his wounds we are healed.
All we like sheep have gone astray;
We have turned—every one—to his own way;
And the Lord has laid on him the iniquity of us all.

Isaiah 53:4–6

While others can be healed and set free through the servant's suffering, it is not black women and girls' responsibility to share this burden. Nevertheless, comparing the suffering servant and black women illustrates the divine connection the two share. The black woman is strong like Jesus, and the black woman is weak like Jesus.

LIVING WITH STRENGTH AND WEAKNESS

We are human; therefore, we are strong *and* weak. Many of us, particularly black women and girls, have not been taught how to graciously give ourselves space to live with weakness. Weakness makes us acknowledge our inabilities and surrender to forces outside of ourselves for help. All of this contradicts our understandings of success and strength. We have difficulty seeing power in weakness.

Some of the worst feelings I ever experience come when I must show up, be present, and be strong when every bone in my body feels weak. In these moments, I desperately want the day, week, or month off from having to be strong. In these moments, my spirit, soul, and mind just need a break. I don't know what God wants me to do then. I don't know how much of God's strength I can use or how much of my own weakness I can bear. I've had so many moments where, like Deborah, I've wondered why God would make me a warrior when I'm really just weak. Sometimes, I feel like I have more shortcomings than strengths. My fallible humanity far outweighs any accolades on my résumé. My weaknesses make me feel isolated and lonely despite the blessing of a great community of people around me.

Then I hear Jesus's words: "Come to me, all of you who are weary and carry heavy burdens, and I will give you rest" (Matthew 11:28). God knows when we are weak and weary and just need rest. God knows how daunting life can be. God knows how fragile our hearts are. God offers us rest so God can take our weaknesses and weariness for God's own self. In our most difficult moments, God is not asking us to push through to strength but rather to surrender our weaknesses to God so God can go from there.

God can be trusted with our weakness and vulnerabilities. Weakness makes us surrender to God. Jesus demonstrated this surrender in the garden of Gethsemane before his subsequent betrayal and arrest. He was weak. His soul was weary. Jesus was tired, "He went a little farther and fell on his face, and prayed, saying "O my Father, if it is possible, let this cup pass from me; nevertheless, not as I will, but as you will," (Matthew 26:39).

We usually focus on the latter part of the scripture where Jesus prays, "nevertheless, not as I will, but as you will." However, Jesus's statement before that was powerful in itself. He says, "Father, if it is possible, let this cup pass from me." He shows us what to do when we find ourselves in our weakest moments. We should go before God and offer our weakness, trusting God knows exactly what to do with it.

Weakness is a part of the human experience just as much as strength. We will never be free of weakness and its presence in our lives altogether. Our weaknesses don't make us any less human or any less of the warriors God has created us to be. We have to learn and grow both through and from our weakness. We have to allow our weaknesses to be our teacher. Weakness allows us to learn new things about ourselves and about our lives.

There is a kind of strength that is almost frightening in black women.
It's as if a steel rod runs right through the head down to the feet.
—Maya Angelou[12]

I saw the image of God in Deborah. She was a warrior. She recognized her identity as a warrior and knew she possessed a unique strength even as a nine-year-old child. However, she also perceived weakness as failure, a liability instead of a part of who she was as a child of God. She thought in order for her life to have any value she had to maintain her warrior strength at all times. Instead of turning to God for strength in her weakness, she resented him *for* her weakness. I had to assure her with the lesson I learned from her powerful question, as well as myself as I continue my journey through life: warriors can be weak and that is okay. Weakness is an inherent part of the human experience. God's love extends from the strongest to the weakest parts of ourselves.

Deborah's struggles as a young black girl wrestling with a perceived mantle of strength reminded me of similar struggles I'd had my entire life. While I marveled at Deborah's courage to ask her question, I later realized I'd had to garner my own courage to respond, to admit warriors can be weak and that I can be weak. I, a strong, independent, black woman, can also be vulnerable and fragile.

Black women have not had permission to be both. We need to be seen for all of who we are. I am proud of the strength in my DNA as a black woman and warrior,:yet I am also grateful for the grace that gives me space to be weak when I need to be.

Deborah made me confront my own weaknesses. I still don't know why God created us to have both weakness and strength. However, as 1 Corinthians suggests, God uses the weak things of the world to shine a light of truth on the strong. God chose to become incarnate in the weakness of Christ in order to present a powerful gospel of truth to the world. Weakness was the chosen one. Therefore, do not discount weakness. God resides with us in both our strength and our weakness; neither limits God.

After a few months, Deborah's mother stopped bringing her to me. I'd like to believe things have gotten better for Deborah. I'd like to believe my words somehow continue to speak to her. I'd like to believe she found a way to navigate her weaknesses and know God is with her. I also hope she can embrace the warrior strength God gave her. My answer was no panacea to her feeling stuck and unwanted, but it dispelled the myth that weakness made us valueless. It freed me, and I hope freed Deborah, from feeling like we, as black women and girls, have to keep a perfect score sheet of strength. This situation reminded me warriors that were human and humans had weak moments. Perhaps God didn't perceive us as weak or strong at all. Perhaps God loved us as our most true and full selves.

Parable of the
INSECURE BROWN GIRL

"If God knew I would feel insecure about my skin and my hair,
then why would he choose to make me born like this?"
—Leah, age nineteen

L eah and I met through a mentoring program at my church when
she was in middle school. It took her some time to embrace the
idea of having or needing a mentor. Leah was a shy and quiet girl
and was cautious about opening up to anyone unfamiliar. Occasional
text messages just to check-in eventually turned to regular Skype
conversations over the next several years. Leah considered her childhood to be full of joyous memories. She came from a loving home
with parents who took care of her and her three siblings.

"My parents are really thoughtful and sensitive," she said happily.
"They always make me feel safe and want the best for me."

Leah often went out of her way to assure me her parents had
always been protective and supportive.

She went to Christian schools growing up and remembered feeling very anxious about the messages she received.

"My teacher called Obama the antichrist," she recalled.

Comments like this bothered her, but she could never determine if they were racist or critical of Obama's politics. Nevertheless, she never felt singled out or ostracized as most of her classmates were black like her.

"Things were pretty normal then," she said.

However, when Leah switched from her small, multiethnic private school to a larger public school, she experienced major culture shock. She was one of very few black students there.

"It was my first time experiencing microaggressions and racism on a daily basis. I didn't know how to deal with the fact other people thought negatively about my skin and my hair. They would make jokes about black stereotypes."

She particularly hated when other students touched her hair without permission. The subtle and blatant disrespect was difficult for Leah to process, so she kept her feelings to herself even though these experiences depressed and weighed on her heavily. Eventually, the negative effects of it all came out in other ways.

Leah suffered from severe anxiety and depression, which subsequently turned to self-harm when she was fourteen years old. The physical effects the self-harm had on her body didn't bother her because she didn't think she was going to be around long and couldn't conceive of a future. Even now, one can see the scars on her frail nineteen-year-old arms. She tried to hide her wounds from her family with adhesive bandages; but since companies typically made those bandages for lighter skin tones, her wounds were difficult to conceal.

Leah couldn't avoid her parents' intuition. "I was cutting, but eventually I couldn't hide it anymore."

When they discovered her scars, they were horrified and scared for their child and immediately took her to a therapist. "I self-harmed because I wanted to see my pain on me," she admitted. While working with her therapist, Leah realized her depression had led to her cutting. She eventually stopped self-harming and then eventually stopped going to therapy.

Though Leah stopped cutting herself, she next developed an eating disorder. She articulately explained the transition as though she had examined the psychology behind her choices:

> I felt out of control based on the fact that I have darker skin and kinkier hair. Every time I looked in the mirror, I felt broken, and I couldn't control those aspects of myself, so I became obsessed with controlling my weight. I noticed when I gained weight that I would feel so much worse about my skin and my hair; but when I lost weight, at least I had this that was good about me.

This time, she went into an intensive day treatment and outpatient program to treat her disorder. However, the atmosphere at the treatment program didn't help her.

"I was surrounded by skinny white girls. My therapist was white. My dietician was white. I didn't want to talk about race or racism because I was the only black girl." As a result, Leah withdrew into herself.

Leah was nervous when she finally mentioned her discomfort with being the only black girl in the facility to her therapist. Her therapist, a white woman, didn't understand but tried to help.

"Sometimes white people say ignorant things without meaning to. She was my therapist but she was also human and I understood that, but it didn't help me."

Again, Leah stopped going to therapy.

She spent the next few years trying to manage her conditions on her own. Sometimes she would self-harm and other times she would go months without doing it at all. Sometimes she wouldn't eat a thing and other times she ate regularly. The cycle was endless.

When Leah enrolled in college, she found herself in a new space with new people, but the same issues plagued her. She was alone again, just like in her high school and day treatment facility, surrounded by crowds of people who did not look like her. One night while at a party, Leah drank far too much, self-harming in a different way. She was rushed to the hospital with alcohol poisoning. The nurses were additionally concerned when they saw her scarred arms and frail body. Leah was taken to an adolescent treatment facility for two weeks—yet another place where she was the only black girl and another place where she encountered racist comments.

"One day, we were lining up for lunch and someone asked where I was. Another girl responded, 'How could you miss her? She's the darkest one here.'"

Wherever she went, the racism and microaggressions followed her.

Upon leaving the adolescent treatment facility, Leah returned to her first intensive day treatment and outpatient program. This time, she successfully prevented the isolating environment from affecting her progress and graduated from the program after a year. She was proud of herself for graduating. She felt her depression and anxiety were getting better. Still, Leah questioned if treatment could ever truly help her.

"I graduated because there wasn't anything else they could do for someone like me."

Since then, Leah has had a few relapses. "It's not so bad to where I need to be hospitalized, but I'm managing." She's less depressed and no longer suicidal, but she admits she hasn't completely addressed her insecurities regarding her skin color and hair.

"If I could conquer those things then I wouldn't need my eating disorder anymore."

Leah recalled meeting a girl in the treatment facility who said God put her through anxiety and depression for a reason. Leah resented that statement.

"If that were the case for me, then I felt like God was playing me. What was the purpose?" she reflects. "If God knew I would feel insecure about my skin and my hair, then why would he choose to make me born like this?"

> *Who taught you to hate the texture of your hair?*
> *Who taught you to hate the color of your skin?*
> —Malcolm X[13]

I remember the first time someone called me the N-word. I remember the first time someone called me "darky." I remember the first time someone called me "nappyhead." These racist moments remain etched in my memory, teaching me from a young age that black girls are undesired and rejected. It has taken me years to renounce these messages and recover from their harmful effects. I'm amazed by how much black women and girls have to unlearn. We are born into a system designed to oppose every aspect of our identity, including our skin complexion, hair, attitude, and overall identity as women. The antagonism we face begins at such a young age and from so many different directions that even the most spiritually, emotionally, and physically protected black girls have a difficult time countering it. As Melissa Harris-Perry writes in book *Sister Citizen: Shame, Stereotypes, and Black Women in America*:

> Black women in America have always had to wrestle with derogatory assumptions about their character and identity. These assumptions shape the social world that black women must accommodate or resist in an effort to preserve their authentic selves and to secure recognition as citizens.[14]

For centuries, prejudice and negative stereotyping have attacked black women and girls' characters and physical natures. Leah is a casualty of this reality, and she is tragically far from alone. Most struggle in silence like Leah does, trying to find a safe home for their identity.

THE ONLY BLACK GIRL

I was born in Brooklyn, NY, in a time when Brooklyn was seemingly 100 percent black American. I honestly don't remember seeing anyone who didn't have dark skin. I was young, so I thought this was normal. Of course, I recall seeing other faces from time to time, whether in person or on my television screen, but it wasn't a *thing*. Being part of a cultural majority was my reality. When one is a member of a majority, one doesn't have to process what it means to be the other, either rationally or emotionally.

My family moved to the New Jersey suburbs when I was in second grade. The grandness of the suburbs fascinated me. Everything seemed so big, including my new school. It seemed there were hundreds and hundreds of students. *And these students looked nothing like me.* I was confused and overwhelmed, and I could not find one person who looked like me. I was lost.

My young mind couldn't process what was happening. Though I felt very different, I still tried to make connections with the people around me. I tried to join in by playing with two white boys on the playground. One was happy to hang out with me, the other protested, "We don't play with n*ggers," already comfortable and conditioned to use racist language.

Other students asked uncomfortable questions like, "Why does your skin get like that?" or "Why does your hair shrivel up like that" or "Can you tan?" At eight years old, I had to educate those around me about different aspects of being a black girl. I went from a carefree childhood experience while being part of a cultural majority to a confusing, pressure-filled, self-doubting childhood experience full of so-called "teachable moments" as the only black girl. I was the only one in my classes, the only one on my team, the only one in class pictures.

I recently asked a few high school girls who attend predominantly white schools how they felt about being one of the few black girls there:

> When I'm in class, I'm the only person of color all the time. I always have to have my guard up but at the same time, I try not to get too annoyed at certain things. —Tenth grade

> You have to be mentally tough. If you're not already mentally tough then it can mess you up. Sometimes I am and sometimes I'm not. But you really can't have any off days. —Tenth grade

> You definitely have to wear two faces when you're the only black girl. You can't say certain things when you're around the white crowds as you would feel comfortable to say when you're around the black crowds. —Twelfth grade

> Whenever we talk about African American history in my history class or English class, everyone would turn and look at me like I'm the only black girl. God forbid we're reading something like *A Raisin in the Sun* or *Othello*. Everyone would turn around to me and ask if I know anything about stuff they had questions about. I'm thinking we're all reading this at the same time and learning at the same time." —Ninth grade

The girls that I interviewed—girls like Leah—haven't been able to find ways to grow from and transcend these spaces to feel comfortable with who they are.

Most people don't understand how being the only one (representing a race, gender, or other demographic) can affect a person psychologically. They assume it's not a big deal. I remember having a conversation with a friend about a minority student's frustrations regarding the lack of representation in leadership on their campus. My friend didn't understand why people couldn't just look past all of that and feel comfortable as human beings. Although he meant well, I pointed out this was easy for him to say as a white male in an institution that was, on paper, only fifty-one percent white, but appeared ninety percent white when walking through campus. I remember what it felt like to be in the majority as a child. Those who are in spaces where they are the majority don't think twice about their personhood; they don't have to do so.

Since that first day of school in second grade, I have been the only black girl in my schools, jobs, clubs, and living communities numerous times. How I navigate these spaces has changed over time, and every challenge now makes me stronger and more self-assured. Young black girls in predominantly nonblack spaces find it difficult to exist because of cultural isolation. They are often left feeling alone and misunderstood. Sometimes they try to blend in, but people single them out negatively. Other times when they do stand out, people encourage them to blend in with everyone else. Often, those who don't ever have these experiences easily dismiss those who do.

BLACKNESS

Leah's struggle with her dark skin is no surprise. Despite the fact that our skin is its own rainbow of brown colors, somewhere along the line our rainbow of brown people became simply "black people." Historically, societies in many different countries use "black" as a racial designation to describe darker-skinned people, but they rarely associate this blackness with goodness and beauty and frequently associate it with negativity, both aesthetically and culturally. These negative connotations of blackness have carried over throughout generations, designed to position lighter-skinned people as superior over darker-skinned people.

Naming encompasses an important part of black culture as black people have sought to reclaim a collective identity. Terms used to describe us has evolved over the centuries: n*gger, negro, colored, Afro-American, black, African American, black American, African-descended, and so on. Additionally, black people have been labeled "minority" and "person of color" (PoC). The 1980s saw a campaign to promote culture-wide usage of the term African American, but it competed with the more recent embrace of "black" due to the influence of the Black Power Movement.[15] Some black people rejected the term "black," citing it limits the variety of colors in the race and embraces the negativity behind the word. They instead preferred other terms like "African American." Others rejected "African American" because it didn't include other cultures of black Americans. In spite of the renaming and reclaiming of collective identity, black people have been unable to escape the negative and adverse associations that come with being "black." Many young black girls aren't aware of all the history behind the term or our community's pursuit to escape its detrimental connotations. They just know people see being black as bad.

In the 1940s, Kenneth and Mamie Clark created "The Doll Test," a series of experiments to study the psychological effects of racism and segregation on black children. They used four different dolls to test black children between the ages of three and seven on their perceptions of race. They asked the children to identify the doll's race and which doll the children preferred. The majority of the children chose the white doll, associating it with positive characteristics, and associating the black doll with negative ones. In subsequent decades, the doll test has been given numerous times. In 2005, Kiri Davis produced a seven-minute documentary called *A Girl Like Me* where she administered the doll test with twenty-one black children. She would ask, "Can you show me the doll that is the nice doll?" Many children would point to the white doll. "And why is that the nice doll?" "Because she's white," one of the children answered. "Can you show me the doll that looks bad?" Davis then asked. Many children pointed to the black doll. "Why does that look bad?" They responded, "Because she's black." Finally, the Davis asked, "Can you give me the doll that looks like you?" All of the children pointed to the black doll.[16]

Black children like Leah or the ones in *A Girl Like Me* psychologically process antiblackness at young ages, having experienced it in various aspects of society and their everyday lives. I have seen this in elementary school classrooms, among their friends, and even in the entertainment they watch. One ten-year-old girl shared with me a time she accidentally bumped into a woman while standing in line at a grocery store with her mother. The woman turned around and said, "Someone get this little n*gger." The girl's mother responded with rage, and the two women argued in the store. The girl said this happened when she was eight years old. These type of experiences can lead to internalized hatred for most black girls. They know they are black and they know blackness bears negative associations; therefore, they naturally associate themselves with that antagonism.

BLACK HAIR

Imagine going through life having to qualify the hair that that sits on top of one's head. Most black girls don't have to imagine; this *is* how they go through life. Melissa Harris-Perry writes, "Black hair might not always be that way, but within the current US context, it is such a defining aspect of the lives of black girls and black women."[17] Many are introduced to this reality at a young age: people touching their hair without permission, questioning the change in length when they take their braids out, or grappling with what it means to have kinky hair.

I had a head full of full, thick hair growing up. Getting my first perm was a thrilling rite of passage. Finally, my hair would be "straight." Only when I got older did I begin to analyze the complex issues with why straight hair was considered the social norm. I had to ask myself why my hair was not acceptable. I questioned what having straight hair meant. I recently asked several teenaged black girls what they consider to be "good hair." Their responses varied:

- Good hair is anything that is straight hair.
- You have to look exotic. It can't shrink towards your head when you shower. And if it does, it has to be 3C loose curls. That's the acceptable natural.
- Good hair to society is long and blonde.
- Bad hair is hair you have to perm or relax.

Many of the girls, however, said they had reclaimed what it means to have good hair in their older age, stating they perceive good hair as healthy hair. Leah didn't talk much about her hair; it was a sensitive topic for her. During one conversation, I noticed she wore her hair in a French braid. I wondered if she did so for style, for convenience, or for tucking it away. I wanted to ask where she was on her hair journey—a black girl's act of moving beyond a Western European perception of hair standards to embrace and accept her own hair. Every black girl has her own hair journey. For some, the hair journey is moving from a place of hair resentment to hair love. In this movement, a black girl realizes she must study and learn about how to care for and nurture her hair. She realizes her hair requires investment and love.

> I grew up in a very white community. My mom is white and didn't know what to do with my hair, so she straightened it a lot. Now it's all damaged. I'm at the point where I want to cut it off. —Fifteen years old

> Even though I don't show my hair because I cover it for my religion, last year I just gave up and chopped off some of my hair with school scissors. My mom permed my hair and since then it was just really

damaged. After I cut it, I've had to really research my hair type. —
Seventeen years old

Something that seems so small, such as walking into a black
beauty supply store or beauty salon, can be such a restorative moment
for a black girl. Something about the experience can feel very much
like coming home. Many of us have spent much of our lives walking
into stores where most of the products aren't meant for our hair.
The products don't have our faces on them, and the advertising and
product language have little relevance for our hair and our culture.
In these black beauty supply stores and beauty salons, everything is
catered to us and our sensibilities.

The movie *Belle* tells the story of Belle, a biracial black woman
raised by a white family in the late 1700s. The movie highlights Belle's
external and internal struggles as a biracial black woman. In one
scene, she cannot get a comb to go through her hair smoothly. Both her
straight-haired white cousin and the family's black maid witness her
struggle as she grows more and more embarrassed. The maid offers
to help and tells Belle she has to start from the bottom and work her
way up. As the maid demonstrates how to use the comb, Belle seems
relieved someone finally understands her and is happy someone, for the
first time, has taught her how to comb her kind of hair.

As I watched that scene, I realized not only did Belle have to learn
how to comb her hair, she also had to unlearn the disdain she had for
her hair too. For many young black girls like Belle or Leah, having
kinky hair is a curse instead of a blessing. The hair journey is all about
loving and accepting our identity as a gift. The fact that black girls
have to go through these journeys at all is bewildering. The majority
of us must go through a lifelong process of learning to love our hair
because we have been conditioned from a young age to hate it.

BLACK WEIGHT

> I noticed when I gained weight that I would feel so much worse about my skin and my hair but when I lost weight, at least I had this that was good about me. —Leah, age nineteen

I loved basketball as a young person growing up. I also hated basketball because of some experiences I endured as one of two black girls on the basketball team. Our high school team was successful and extremely competitive, and my coach had very high standards for our preparedness when it came to playing. Every preseason we worked out daily as a team, conditioning to get ourselves physically fit for the season ahead. I hated preseason conditioning for one reason: weigh-ins. We had one weigh-in at the beginning of our preseason conditioning and one at the end to see how much weight we had either lost or sustained. I recall our coach and assistant coach would gather all of the girls into one room and weigh us individually in front of one another. I dreaded hearing my name called and what number would be on the scale after I stepped onto it. All of the girls on the team were skinny white girls with little to no muscle mass. I, on the other hand, was a little heavier than the rest of them. I had more curves, bigger hips and a bigger rear-end. I also had a bigger chest and I could never quite find the right sports bra to support my size, so I wore two sports bras for games and practices.

I would eat very little, if at all, in the days ahead of the weigh-ins. I would feel fear and nervousness when I stepped on the scale, hearing my coach read my weight out loud and commenting in front of everyone that I was too heavy and needed to lose weight. My coach's disappointment would be loud in his tone too. The assistant coach would write the number down onto her pad as I walked over to the other girls, embarrassed and ashamed. For the rest of preseason training, I would do the same weight training as the other girls and run the same distances, but I just could not lose the pounds. I tried going on a cabbage diet and looking up other ways to drop weight before the next weigh-in. Sometimes, I would have lost maybe one or two pounds by that final weigh-in, or my weight just stayed the same. Other times, I would have gained a few more pounds, probably of muscle mass due to all of the weight lifting. When that happened, I would come up with an excuse, usually telling him it was my time of the month so I carried a little more weight. He'd express his same disappointment, though, as if I hadn't been working as hard as the other girls.

One time in particular, the girl ahead of me to get weighed was a very thin white girl. He jokingly called her "spaghetti noodle." Everyone laughed pleasantly, including the girl. When I came forward, he jokingly called me "beef-a-roni" and everyone laughed. I did too, but not pleasantly. This was psychological torture for me as a fifteen-year-old girl. My body was shaped differently than all of the other girls and I did not know why. I felt "othered" for being one of only a handful of black girls in my majority-white public school in the 1990s. For the most part, the black girls there were all trying to fit in, so we weren't friends with one another and could not share these experiences. I went through mine alone, suffering in silence like Leah. Only grace kept me from having an eating disorder or using other forms of self-harm.

Recently, one of the girls I teach at my school was having a conversation with her friends and I overheard her say she didn't like her hair or her weight. She didn't like her hair because she thought it was too thin and kinky, and she did not quite know how to style it. She didn't like her weight because she thought she was too heavy. Then she followed up her confession by saying she knew she shouldn't feel this way because even though she weighed more than others, she was 5'9" and a black girl.

"Black girls just have different body types. This is something that I know," she said. "I know we have bigger butts and thighs and stuff. It's still hard, though."

Her friends affirmed her, saying she had a beautiful body type and she should not feel insecure about it. They were the sounding board and community she needed to encourage her. As I listened, I had to wonder how things would have been different for me as a fifteen-year-old if I could've articulated and worked through my own insecurities with an affirming community of sisters.

> So God created human beings in his own image. In the image of God he created them; male and female he created them.
>
> —Genesis 1:27 NLT

IMAGO DEI

God never intended for us to hate the way we look. God never intended for us to see people as less or as something negative, something *other*. We are created in God's image and likeness. We are intended to represent the unique aspect of God. Black women's skin and hair, like mine and Leah's, are rare illustrations of God's image. We are all God's gift to the earth and the beautiful embodiment of the *imago Dei*.

Imago Dei, a theological term rooted in Genesis 1:27, says human beings are created in the image and likeness of God. While this is a fascinating concept, humans have struggled to conceptualize what it truly means as it relates to themselves as individuals and other humans and living creatures. There are many different interpretations of *imago Dei*; some suggest it grants human beings dominion over the earth or that it reflects human beings' rational nature while others define it as human beings having an actual physical resemblance to God.[18] Many *imago Dei* interpreters reject the notion of human beings and their physical resemblance to God. They contend that overemphasizing physicality can lead to ascribing human attributes to God, which can limit our understanding of God to a particular image. Western interpretations have been limiting in their depictions of God's image, generally reducing it to a singular white male figure. However, all human beings, with all of our differences, reflect God's image. This diversity shows God's image is multidimensional and filled with an immeasurable medley, not limited by one interpretation.

Beyond the physical image, the reflection of God's nature is an important factor of the *imago Dei*. Christian theologian, Daniel Migliore thoroughly analyzes the *imago Dei* in his book *Faith Seeking Understanding: An Introduction to Christian Theology*, writing, "Human life depends upon ecological systems and structures of interrelationship. Stated briefly, we live in dialogue. Long before we are conscious of that fact, we exist in response to and interaction with others."[19] This means our flourishing as human beings depends on our ability to live in connection with each other. We can also learn more about God through this interconnection. There is a short poem, often attributed to William Blake, that says, "I sought my God and my God I couldn't find / I sought my soul and my soul eluded me / I sought to serve my brother in his need, and I found all three / My God, my soul, and thee."

Martin Luther King Jr. quoted this poem often when trying to get people to look beyond their racial prejudices and see God within one another. Migliore goes on to say community is the clue to our human identity,[20] and I would add it's the clue to God's identity as well. If human beings are made in the image of God, then the way we learn about God and God's nature is through living in community with one another.

Black girls are made in the image of God. While this shouldn't be a revolutionary statement, it is because of how rarely people acknowledge this fact. Black girls hear far more messages about how their aesthetic falls short of traditional beauty standards than they hear about how they embody God's image. Even the more-accepted black girls get qualifiers like "pretty for a black girl," suggesting their beauty is notable among other black girls, but not for girls in general. Black girls' hair, skin, and bodies are constantly under a microscope and are usually considered inferior. In failing to value black girls, we miss an essential part of God's image.

In 2007, Canadian author William P. Young published *The Shack*, a novel about a man who experiences a tragedy that leads him to a divine encounter with three strangers. The leader of the three strangers is a woman called "Papa" who fulfills the symbolic role of God. While *The Shack* isn't perfect, the choice to illustrate God as a curvy black woman is significant. In one part of the novel, the main character questions his perception of God:

> Was one of these people God? What if they were hallucinations or angels, or God was coming later? That could be embarrassing. Since there were three of them, maybe this was a Trinity sort of thing. But two women and a man and none of them white? Then again, why had he naturally assumed that God would be white?[21]

Many influential Christian leaders call *The Shack* incorrect, dangerous, and heretical. "It misrepresents God," one pastor has said.[22] There is a strong correlation between *The Shack*'s physical depiction of God and these criticisms. In the film adaptation, actress Octavia Spencer played the role of God. More controversy over God being a black woman ensued. Joe Schimmel, pastor of Blessed Hope Chapel in Simi Valley, California, said:

> Young's pretentious caricature of God as a heavy set, cushy, non-judgmental, African American woman called "Papa" (who resembles the New Agey Oprah Winfrey far more than the one true God revealed

through the Lord Jesus Christ—Heb 1:1–3) . . . lends itself to a dangerous and false image of God and idolatry.[23]

In contrast, people seldom question Hollywood films and artwork traditionally depicting God as older, white, and male. Traditional images depicting this singular "image of God" are rarely considered heretical. On the other hand, I have seen images of God depicted as black, Mexican, or even as a woman, and each time they were considered controversial or heretical. Dorothy Sayers addresses the typical depiction of God in her book *The Mind of the Maker*. She gives her own analysis of the phrase "image of God" from the passage in Genesis 1:

> The expression "in His own image" has occasioned a good deal of controversy. Only the most simple-minded people of any age or nation have supposed the image to be a physical one. The innumerable pictures which display the Creator as a hirsute old gentleman in flowing robes seated on a bank of cloud are recognized to be purely symbolic. The "image," whatever the author may have meant by it, is something shared by male and female alike; the aggressive masculinity of the pictorial Jehovah represents power, rationality, or what you will: it has no relation to the text I have quoted.[24]

Sayers challenges us to view God beyond gender. She challenges us to perceive the image of God as reflected in all of humanity. Young accepted this challenge with *The Shack*.

The controversial response to the image of God as a black woman helps illustrate why the message of the *imago Dei* has not been received by some groups, particularly black women and girls. If people consider an image of God as a black woman harmful and heretical, then *imago Dei* is not for everyone. If people can only envision God as male and white, then *imago Dei* is not for everyone. In her own way, Leah's initial question echoes this false idea: What was the purpose in God creating her if God knew she would feel insecure about herself?

God *did* have a purpose in creating Leah in God's image, but unfortunately, larger society has failed her by excluding black girls and rejecting their aesthetic.

Imago Dei must be more than an ideological concept. It has to be practical for everyone, especially those who are not getting the message. It is more than simply, "how we view others." *Imago Dei* must translate to spiritual practice, the intentional discipline people engage to develop spiritually. Spiritual practices are designed to bring us closer to God and thus be transformed into more connected human beings—connected to God, connected to one another, and connected to ourselves. For black girls like Leah, *imago Dei* can be an intentional practice of engaging them as one would honor God. By engaging black girls as the *imago Dei*, we connect deeper to ourselves, to one another, and to God.

Practicing *imago Dei* profoundly impacts how we treat others. Our own perception of God and our care of others are directly related. In the Gospels, Jesus, when asked to name the greatest commandment, responds, "Love the Lord your God with all your heart and with all your soul and with all your mind" (Matthew 22:37). And Jesus proclaims the second-greatest commandment is "to love your neighbor as yourself" (Mark 12:31). Girls like Leah are our neighbor and we are to love girls like her with the same care, respect, compassion, and concern as we would ourselves. As a society, we have failed to recognize and honor the *imago Dei* of black women and girls. Adopting an *imago Dei* practice with our local neighbors, and more specifically, the black girls in our communities, is a commandment of God.

We are all created by God in God's likeness. The false notion that only one particular type of person reflects God's image causes irreparable damage to black girls. The *imago Dei* is not exclusive, and we must be held accountable for allowing that bias to pervade. Girls like

Leah need to know they, with their kinky, curly hair and black skin, are an express reflection of God's creative genius.

> *Sometimes black women can conquer negative*
> *myths, sometimes they are defeated,*
> *and sometimes they choose not to fight.*
> —Melissa Harris-Perry[25]

The tragedy of Leah's parable is that even now she has been unable to find a safe space in which she can thrive. In most of her environments, she has to qualify her skin, her hair, and her existence. I empathize with Leah's experience as I have had to qualify the same aspects of myself my entire life. Many black girls find themselves in similar predicaments. Because of this, black girls must find ways to cope with few tools to do so in a healthy way. Leah's way of coping with her depression and anxiety manifested into self-harm.

I contemplate who Leah would be had she been born into a society where her black skin and kinky hair were embraced. I question how effective a few encouraging voices can be in a world infused with negative messages about her being. I wonder who Leah would be had she gone to a school where her peers accepted her as equal, marveled at the beauty of her skin, and kept their hands out of her hair. I think about the opportunities her white therapists had to research, ask questions, and explore how they could've provided the best environment to care for black girls like Leah. Black girls have challenges specific to them and cannot be lumped into an "all girls" category. Leah didn't have any of those avenues of escape so she had to find her own way.

I caught up with Leah over video conferencing while she was in London on an exchange program with her school.

"Do you see God in your story?" I asked.

"I am by no means healed," Leah responded, "but I have encountered other people who relate to my story who are black girls and they've said to me, 'Oh my gosh I've never met another black girl who has had these issues. It's always other white girls.' I do see God in that. Being able to heal others as I'm healing myself."

Leah has come to terms with why God made her with her unique features. She still struggles, but she no longer resents God for it.

"I don't feel that resentment anymore," she said in a later conversation. "I realized we can't comprehend why God does things. It still makes me upset from time to time." As I reminded Leah she is the *imago Dei*, she responded with a confidence I had not ever seen in her.

"God is a black woman."

I asked her to elaborate.

"Well, it's kinda like the whole thing with Jesus having to go through suffering for humankind in order for him and us to be raised to something higher. I feel like since black women have had to carry the world on their shoulders and suffer, how could God not be a black woman?"

Parable of the
THE VOICELESS
BROWN GIRL

*"If my words aren't important, or my feelings or
my personhood, then why am I here?"*
—Lyric, age sixteen

yric's voice was deep and monotonous for a sixteen-year-old girl.
When she spoke, one could hear the maturity in her timbre. Her
vocal tones held the sound of someone who had lived a challenging life and had wisdom to share.

Lyric and I met the summer after she attended a weeklong class
for Vacation Bible School at my church. Her grandmother, whom
Lyric was visiting for the summer, had enrolled her. We periodically
met throughout the rest of the summer, chatting on a bench outside
the church at dusk after a long day at the camp where she worked.
She always accessorized her hot-pink camp T-shirt with silver hoop
earrings and a multicolored scarf wrapped around her head to cover

her hair. She always said she was too busy to do her hair and the scarf was more convenient to wear. One particular day I noticed that her face looked tired and forlorn.

"It's been a long day," she said. "A long life."

Lyric didn't speak a word until she was four years old. "The doctors thought that I was going to be autistic. But I'm here and I'm blessed."

The first words she spoke were lines from the movie, *The Wiz*. "I sang the song 'Don't Nobody Bring Me No Bad News.'"[26] She laughed to herself and sang the song. She still knew all the words. While a fun and catchy song, it also spoke to Lyric's life. Despite Lyric's positivity, life had brought her one set of bad news after the other.

Lyric had been bullied all through fifth and sixth grade. Her peers harassed her by saying, "You sound like a man." Occasionally, they threw rocks at Lyric, and at one point she even received hate mail.

"People would write letters and leave [them] at my house and tell me I should kill myself. I would tell my teachers and stuff, but no one believed me."

At one point, someone created an "I Hate Lyric" Instagram page. Students posted pictures of Lyric and took turns commenting about her looks and sharing gossip. When this happened, she thought she finally had the evidence to give to her school's principal.

"All [the bullies] got was suspended," she lamented. "But after a while, I handled it and made it stop. I'd cuss them out. I would throw hands. I just didn't care. You not gonna mess with me and get away with it."

Lyric started fighting more and more in schools, and administrators suggested to her parents to get Lyric an evaluation.

"They thought I was bipolar because of my anger and because I had a lot of energy. I went to a psychiatrist and he told me I had borderline personality disorder." After being on medication for a few months, the side effects made Lyric feel drowsy and increased her anxiety and depression. She eventually took herself off the medication without her parents realizing it and committed to fighting less and being a calmer a person.

"I realized later violence isn't really the answer, and I had to reevaluate myself and who God made me to be."

After that decision, Lyric's life went in a positive direction. Her grades improved and she didn't get into much trouble. While the bullying subsided only a little, she vowed not to let the "haters" get to her. Lyric was learning to live contentedly. These favorable moments changed one summer day when she was fourteen years old.

"I was molested," she revealed somberly.

Lyric explained the day with vivid memory. She was at her god-brother's house with her cousin, and the three were watching a movie. Her cousin left early, but Lyric stayed to finish watching.

Out of nowhere, he came on to me. I said no, but he ripped my shirt. I kept pushing and telling him no and we started fighting. He actually laughed. He thought it was a joke! I just remember him having me in a choke hold. I fought him off as much as I could but he was too strong. I sat there for a minute and took it but then when he didn't expect it, I fought him off and then ran home.

Lyric immediately went into the shower, desperately trying to wipe away his smell. She wondered what she should do and decided to tell one of her family members. Lyric recalled the disappointing reaction.

"You know how she responded? 'You better not be lying,' is what she said."

Lyric didn't bother telling anyone else after that. Once again, she was in a situation where she didn't think anyone would believe her.

"I think I became depressed [again] after because if my words aren't important, my feelings or my personhood, then why am I here? Why am I alive?"

In the months that followed, Lyric experienced suicidal thoughts with depression. She kept to herself, thinking that no one cared. Eventually, she tried to confide in another family member.

"I remember telling my sister I was going to overdose. I'm not sure if she thought I was lying, but she didn't care."

No matter where she turned, Lyric felt alone. She told me she felt so much pain that she just wanted to die, and she wanted to control her death.

"I didn't want to wait till God called me home."

One evening, she wrapped an iron cord around her neck. "I couldn't breathe, and then I blacked out. I remember seeing a light and then I don't know what happened after that."

When her mother and sister found her goodbye letters to them in the house, they rushed to her room where they found her and frantically tried to get her conscious. When they felt her heartbeat, they were relieved Lyric was still alive.

"They acted like they cared but it was bullshit," she said.

They immediately took her to the hospital; when she was discharged from there, they sent her to a psychiatric center where she stayed for three weeks.

Those three weeks were torture. I was locked up in a room for hours and hours. I had to take shots. I didn't know what they were doing to me. I didn't know why I was taking the pills. I just wanted to get out of there so I said anything I had to say to get out.

Lyric often reflects on why she is still alive. Whereas before she thought God had more important things to do than care for her, she's now convinced that's not true.

God is the only reason I'm still on this earth. He really brought me through so many things. I'm not really a churchy-type person, I mean, but I believe in God. I remember going to church one day and

I went to the altar after and I cried to God to take this away from me. God heard my voice, heard my cries. God saved me.

There is a timbre of voice that comes from not being heard and knowing you are not being heard noticed only by others not heard for the same reason.
—Audre Lorde[27]

From birth, Lyric had a hard time finding her voice, both literally and figuratively. When she did find her voice, it developed into a very distinct sound, and her peers had difficulty embracing its uniqueness. Because they didn't understand her voice, they ridiculed it. Additionally, people mistrusted Lyric's voice when it mattered the most. The people around Lyric did not give her the space to speak her truth, nor the benefit of the doubt when she revealed her assault. She spent the majority of her sixteen years neither heard nor believed. While being silenced is a reality of all women, the systems of both patriarchy and racism doubly silence black women and girls. Young black girls like Lyric struggle with owning their voices because contemporary society devalues them and their words.

Most of the students I teach are white. There is a black girl named Kelly in one of my classes and a black girl named Shawn in another. I have watched carefully how the two navigate being the only black girl in those spaces and noted the distinctive manner in which they use their voices. Kelly, not known usually for timidity, is very quiet in class and only speaks when someone calls on her. I intentionally encourage her to speak out more in class. Though she hesitates to contribute to the discussion, it is also clear to me she does have something to say. As I have continued to embolden her, Kelly has progressively become more vocal, but I can still see how difficult it is for her to assert herself.

In the other class, Shawn is the direct opposite. She contributes to class discussions with confidence, knowing what she has to say is important and eagerly sharing with her classmates and me. She tends to raise her voice above the class in order to be heard, speaking louder if others talk over her when she's making a comment. Often, if Shawn does not feel heard, she expresses her frustration with her classmates, making others perceive her as combative. I do continue to encourage her to speak, but I also try to guide her into communicating in ways where she will truly be heard. Nevertheless, I completely understand why she feels she must raise her voice.

Each girl's way of communicating in my classes represents common tactics black girls use to both find and validate their voices within oppressive systems. Because of their collective experiences, black girls innately understand their voices will usually be unheard and misunderstood. As a result, they enter into spaces with this in mind and automatically begin to figure out how they are going to maneuver their voices so they will be heard. Black girls like Lyric, Kelly, and Shawn are challenged with having to find and embrace their voices while simultaneously defending their right to be heard.

MISUNDERSTOOD VOICES

Black girls have distinct characteristics that people around them generally misunderstand. Specifically, these characteristics reflect their persona and identity. Like Lyric and people's negative responses to her deep, mature voice, black girls and women have been boxed into harmful stereotypes and situations that follow them most of their life.

Loud Black Girls

In 2015, eleven black women were kicked off of a train in Napa Valley because they were "laughing too loudly."[28] The women, all part of a book club, were enjoying themselves on their vacations as they were approached by staff on the train and told to quiet down or leave. After continuing their conversation, they were told they were being escorted off the train for laughing and talking too loudly. Humiliated and embarrassed, the women walked through the train cars and saw police officers waiting for them when they left the train. All they'd been doing was having a good time, but the train staff considered their enjoyment disruptive and noisy. The women filed an $11 million lawsuit against the train company, citing racial bias. This incident sparked the hashtag #LaughingWhileBlack on Twitter.

Similarly, in 2016 Feminista Jones began the hashtag #LoudBlackGirls on Twitter to highlight the silencing of black women, tweeting:

> I think about how we silence ourselves to avoid the "Angry Black Woman" stereotype when we really just need to be heard. . . . I heartily encourage Black girls and women to be as loud and vocal and "ratchet" and "ghetto" and whatever else they say #LoudBlackGirls.[29]

Many black women and girls followed with their own tweets using the #LoudBlackGirls hashtag to reclaim the stereotype. "Maybe we wouldn't have to be so loud if the world actually made an effort to hear us," one woman wrote.[30] Another woman tweeted, "Black women will always be too loud for a world that never intended on hearing us." [31] This same sentiment pervaded hundreds of tweets; black women raise their voices because no one listens to them. "Loud" has developed into a stereotype associated with black women to mischaracterize them as loose cannons. Their loudness is considered unruly and rambunctious. Instead of recognizing black women and girls' voices as powerful tools, people perceive them as problematic. When black girls have to spend a significant part of their lives combating or suppressing this unique part of their existence, they never truly have the space to embrace their own unique voice.

We must remove the negative connotations associated with loudness and reclaim what makes this loudness in black girls special. Loudness is a way some black women and girls communicate lovingly with one another. I grew up with a large extended family from both my mother and my father. My aunts on both sides have very distinct personalities, though I'm especially close to my maternal aunts. While they are different from one another in their personas and passions, they are all very loud when they get together. Growing up, we spent our holidays together, meeting in someone's home to gather for family time. Everyone could hear my aunts, the Clark Sisters, loud and clear no matter where one was in the house. The Clark Sisters laughed loudly, telling stories and talking about the various happenings in the family. My siblings and cousins could all be together in one room and we would cringe when one of the Clark Sisters would scream one of our names to call us in the room to do them a favor. Even now when we get together for holidays as adults, the house is just as noisy and full of love as ever before. I have grown to appreciate the vocal way my family communicates with one another as our language of love.

I notice this same affectionate, loud speech among black women and girls in other settings as well. I hold a conference every year for girls called The Becoming Conference and I set aside space in the schedule so the girls can spend time together beyond the conference programming. Every year during these times, the girls choose to listen to music, dance, take selfies and photos of one another, and just spend time together in general. The room is typically very loud with girls conversing and laughing. Their loudness is *how* they have a good time together and how they express their love for one another. In these moments, their loudness is not a defense mechanism or a plea to be heard, but rather a shared love language. It is important we accept this as part of who they are rather than label it as a problem that needs fixing. Outside of safe spaces like these, most black girls cannot express the fullness of their voices without being silenced, forced to raise their voices with frustration instead of joy to be heard in a world that refuses to listen.

Black Girl with an Attitude

In the same manner loudness should be reclaimed as a distinct part of the language of black women and girls, the "black girl with an attitude" stereotype needs transformation. In my experience, the most prevalent misconception black girls face is "having an attitude." While some black girls can avoid the loud stereotype by just staying quiet, most cannot avoid the attitude one. A fourteen-year-old girl described people's opinions toward her at school, stating, "It doesn't matter what I do here, I am doing it with an attitude." I could relate to her because as a young girl, people constantly thought I had an attitude at school and wherever else I was in the minority.

"Attitude" is another antagonistic characterization that follows black girls and women for most of our lives. Working at predominantly white institutions for the majority of my career, I have seen firsthand the way people respond to black girls' unique personality traits. Because black girls are so often misunderstood, white peers and adults respond negatively to them.

I have lost count of how often other staff accuse these girls of "having an attitude" or "rolling their eyes." I have seen numerous disciplinary reports about black girls where the faculty writes phrases like, "she has a bad attitude"; "I am tired of her attitude"; or "she gives me so much attitude." I have noticed "attitude" is used disproportionately with black girls than nonblack girls, even when the behavior is the same. When faculty writes up nonblack girls, they get phrases like, "but she is a good kid"; "something must be going on with her"; "she's not normally like this"; or "she has just been angry as of late." There is a certain grace given to those girls black girls simply do not get.

Black girls' perceived attitudes are likened to insubordination and lack of discipline. In the times that black girl attitudes are not portrayed explicitly negative, nonblack people, and sometimes even black men, jokingly adopt black girls' mannerisms as a way of relating to black women and girls. Oftentimes unintentionally, these moments quickly become patronizing at best. I recall walking into work one day and a white woman said, "Hey, girlfriend!" in greeting. When my "Hey" wasn't excited enough for her, she placed a hand on her hip and tilted her head to the side, saying, "What's with the attitude this morning, girl?" Even though *her* greeting was the inappropriate one, since she'd put on a stereotypical black woman's voice and mannerisms, *my* normal reply was being chastised. Unfortunately, I had to explain to my coworker I was not giving her an attitude and why I would seem short with her in the early-morning hours. Black women must constantly qualify their responses and behaviors as neutral human reactions with no "attitude" present.

What many perceive as attitude should be interpreted as a distinct aspect of black girls' temperament shaped by generational and sociocultural contexts. Jacqueline B. Koonce argues "talking with an attitude" is a practice within the African American women's speech community.[32] It is an intercultural language shared among one another. Identifying black girls' attitudes as a speech practice is a radical and intentional way of acknowledging their unique personalities. Koonce also suggests black girls' attitudes are a form of communication that allows them to resist oppression and disrespect from those around them. Overall, "speaking with attitude" is a communication mode that is comfortable for black girls and a style people should regard with mindfulness, not mock or label negatively.

Deceitful Black Girls

"I just didn't believe them. . . . The way they dress, the way they act. I didn't like them."[33]

A juror from the R&B singer R. Kelly's 2008 child pornography trial admitted this in an interview ten years after the trial, in the Lifetime documentary, *Surviving R. Kelly*. Kelly was being tried for the alleged sexual abuse of a fourteen-year-old girl. In this brief explanation of his decision, the juror summarizes a pervading cultural sentiment toward black women and girls: he just didn't believe them. He did not believe the eyewitness testimonies and victim accounts because he did not like their dress and behavior. Many of these survivors told their stories in the documentary. They had been abused sexually, physically, and emotionally, and most of this abused began in their teenage years. One question drove the online and offline conversation about R. Kelly and the documentary: should we believe these women? The fact that people could question these women's honesty disturbed me to my core. The documentary recounted testimony after testimony from women of all different ages and backgrounds across decades with near-identical accounts of their abuse. Yet like the juror in Kelly's 2008 trial, many just did not believe the women, echoing pop culture's overall mistrust for years as Kelly's behavior and career continue unscathed and unpunished.

Chance the Rapper's candid apology for making music with Kelly during 2018 interview, which was featured in the documentary, sparked more debate: "But black women are . . . exponentially [a] higher oppressed and violated group of people . . . just in comparison to the whole world," he said. "Maybe I didn't care because I didn't value the accusers' stories . . . because they were black women."[34] He went on to say bigger celebrities were often accused of things and people only noticed when the alleged victims were white women or lighter-skinned women of color. The women accusing Kelly were mostly darker-skinned black women. Chance the Rapper received backlash for the last part of the quote;[35] and though people were really angry about his confession, it was a painful reality we needed to hear. Even well-respected black men could mistrust black women and girls.

"They didn't believe me" is a statement I often hear from black girls. Lyric struggled with people not believing her for her entire life. Even her family members did not believe her when she was molested. I suspect the adultification of black girls affects their believability because their perceived need for less protection, support, and nurturing makes them seem less virtuous. Even in situations where black girls share their truth, their supposed maturity makes people hold these girls accountable for whatever happens to them, as if they should have been able to control the unfortunate situations. Black girls do not have the grace or excuse of youth or vulnerability.[36]

FINDING HER VOICE

In *Counseling Women: A Narrative, Pastoral Approach*, Christie Cozad Neuger establishes a profound definition of what it means for women to come into their voices:

> When I use the term *voice*, I am not just talking about a willingness to speak. I am also talking about the ability to find language and models that validate one's own experience and communicate a sense of entitlement to that experience as authentic and important.[37]

A woman's voice is one of the most important assets that she has. When a woman uses that God-given ability to speak, powerful things can happen.

Whether as a college chaplain, minister, or counselor, one thing I love about my profession is helping women and girls come into and evolve their own voices. It has been a privilege to watch a young woman finally discover how powerful and valuable her voice is and blossom in that knowledge. Nancy Lammers Gross, professor of speech communication in ministry at Princeton Theological Seminary, writes the following about teaching women to find their voices in preaching:

> In my speech classes, we begin by learning how to use the physical voice. In order to use the voice, women must feel that it is theirs to use; they must own it. And to own it, they need to know what it is and how it works.[38]

We need to encourage girls to learn how to value and use their voices every day. It's only when they grow in confidence in these voices that we may begin to see these girls thriving in various areas of their lives.

It starts with black girls practicing owning their voices. I once counseled a ten-year-old girl every week for half-hour sessions. During one session, we played a game where one person pulled a question out of a box unseen and asked it to the other person. The questions ranged from, "What is your most fun memory?" to "If you could change anything about your life, what would it be?" One of my questions to her was, "What are five words you think most describe you?" She paused as though no one had ever asked her that question. She needed time to think about it so we sat quietly for a few minutes.

Before our sessions, people around this young girl labeled her as having an attitude, or "bad," for most of her life. Now she had an opportunity to take charge of her own narrative, not only think about how she felt about herself, but also to voice it. She finally decided on three terms. "Charming, super cute, confident," she declared and beamed. I asked her for the last two, but she was stuck. Nevertheless, she was proud she came up with those three. The following week, she returned but still hadn't figured out the last two. In this session, I helped her think of "smart" and "funny." I noticed she was having a hard time voicing them about herself. Perhaps it was so difficult because these were not words people had allowed her to apply to herself. I saw this as an opportunity for me to give her that language *and* that permission: "You are smart and you are funny." Afterward, she admitted the activity had been difficult for her, but it had also been fun.

Because of how often society constrains and silences them, black girls have to practice using their voices in the most common spaces. I don't mean speaking with a lack of respect for and others, but rather communicating confidently and effectively, realizing they can and should. Most girls I work with have difficulty asserting themselves in their classrooms, social circles, or even homes with their parents and guardians. Yet these are the perfect, everyday spaces where they can practice speaking up, saying what's important to them, giving their opinions, articulating a boundary, and any other ways their voices can assert their identity and well-being. It is imperative for girls, particularly girls of color, to know their voices matter.

"Listen as Wisdom calls out! Hear as understanding raises her voice. . . . Listen to me! For I have important things to tell you. Everything I say is right, for I speak the truth and detest every kind of deception."

—Proverbs 8:1, 6–7

Women's voices have been silenced for centuries, but now many have embraced the importance of women's voices in sacred and public settings. At the end of her story, Lyric realized God had heard her voice all along, concluding her voice was important enough for God's attention, and began a journey to discover how God intended to use her voice. Lyric's insight reflects the Wisdom in Proverbs 8, as well as illustrates what we can glean about women's voices from such passages.

WISDOM IS *SHE*

Proverbs 8 is a powerfully expressive passage that highlights the voice and presence of Wisdom. God used Wisdom to establish the origins of the heavens and the earth. The chapter describes Wisdom as a reflection of God's divine image and an attribute of God's words. Because of this description, many argue Wisdom is part of God's divine nature.

Wisdom's presence in this passage is significant for many reasons, but particularly for Wisdom's personification as female. Wisdom's presenting as female speaks to God's image and character being reflected within women and girls and heard in their voices. Wisdom is the part of God that God placed inside women.

Embodied Wisdom demands to be heard, going out into the hills and calling out into the city: "I call to you, to all of you! I raise my voice to all people" (Proverbs 8:4). In Proverbs 8:6–7, she declares her words are important and true, yet there are people who reject her invitation. Wisdom next qualifies her position by explaining why people should listen, citing her role as God's first creation and then standing alongside God at the foundations of the earth. Proverbs 8 ends with Wisdom again imploring people to listen to her.

Wisdom's consistent beseeching in Proverbs 8 reflects women's continual struggle for their voices to be heard within patriarchal culture. This passage also affirms the role of women's voices as both prophet and preacher. Wisdom is prudent, full of knowledge, and possesses an uncanny discernment. She reflects many of the women and girls that I know. Lyric's voice embodied Wisdom. This young lady's maturity and knowledge seemed to extend far beyond her years. If Wisdom's presence suggests that women possess an important dynamic within their nature, then girls like Lyric inhabit that same nature. We must pay attention. Unfortunately, because she is young, black, and a girl, people diminish their willingness to hear her words. Wisdom, however, demands attention no matter what vessel it comes out of. Wisdom is not just reserved for the educated or the elite, but resides in those whose life experience has shaped their ability to process practical knowledge. Lyric had just that, and God heard her voice and wisdom. Her wisdom was not only in articulating her situations, but also in her ability to glean from each experience regardless of the pain or joy associated with it.

WISDOM SPEAKS

Lyric continues to use her voice in spite of the rejection she faces in the same way Wisdom continued to speak in spite of people constantly dismissing her. Lyric's wisdom and confidence regarding God hearing her teach me that God intentionally gives us voices as instruments to speak. Though difficult, we cannot allow our personal insecurities and external intimidations in our environments sway us from owning and using them.

In 2011, I moved to California to take a new position at Azusa Pacific University as an Associate Campus Pastor for Preaching. Everything about that experience was exciting and intimidating. While I felt blessed to be there, I did not feel prepared. I felt like everyone had more experience than me in this academic environment. They seemed smarter and used new language I'd never heard in any professional settings. I felt like an impostor, so even though my position was a preacher, I decided to observe and be in the background. During my first few weeks, my supervisor called several staff meetings to plan chapels, talk through various situations with students, and brainstorm new programs that we were going to create. After one or two staff meetings of not speaking, my supervisor noted of my silence. He then asked me to stay after a meeting one day, saying he noticed I hadn't been speaking much during the staff meetings. I admitted to him that I didn't feel like I had much to contribute and I just wanted to sit back for a while.

"But I didn't hire you to sit back," he said. "I hired you to speak."

His words sit with me as I practice using my voice in spaces where I don't feel qualified or navigate various environments. Whenever I'm afraid to use my voice, I hear the words, "I hired you to speak." God used my supervisor to remind me of my calling. The Holy Spirit speaks those words us when we limit our voices and sit back on our gifts and the work God has called us to do. God doesn't want us to stay silent. God didn't give us a mouth for us not to use it.

Even the silence has a story to tell you. Just listen. Listen.
—Jacqueline Woodson[39]

Lammers Gross wrote about her experience asking for and listening to women's stories, realizing there were layers underneath women's struggles to use their voices. She wrote, "I came to learn that nearly every woman had a story related to her voice, and that it was important that I listen not only to her physical voice, but also to the story that voice was telling."[40] In the same manner, I learned every young black girl has a story behind her voice. My experience with Lyric taught me that we must listen to black women and girls as though we are listening to God's Wisdom. Unfortunately, we spend more time labeling than learning from girls like Lyric.

Today, Lyric considers herself a content teenager who is still trying to figure out how to use her wise instrument. Lyric's voice, however, continues to be difficult to use because she spends a great deal of time defending herself. She essentially has to encourage herself *by* herself; therefore, her self-doubt frequently overshadows her confidence. She has to raise her voice against the opposition she faces in her personal life and as a young black girl in a contentious culture.

"I don't think I ever get an opinion. Always in the background. Never in the forefront," she laments. Yet, there is hope in her tone. Lyric has faith God hears her voice and because of that, she chooses to press forward. "I'm that lady in Scripture that is like, 'If I can touch the hem of his garment, then I'm okay.' If I can touch, him, then I know I'm good."

Black girls like Lyric desperately try to exercise their voices while also having to defend the tone, style, and manner in which they use that voice. Instead of viewing these aspects of who they are as remarkable parts of their being, society views them as unhinged and unreliable. Society is wrong. The divine Wisdom of God is inherent in each girl; and in Proverbs 8, this Wisdom reminds us she perseveres despite people rejecting her, certain of her voice's significance. Wisdom constantly reminds people if they find her, they will find life. We must listen to these girls in the same manner we must listen to Wisdom.

With God, all things are possible. Because of Lyric's conviction that God hears her and the Wisdom's call in Proverbs 8, I am encouraged to use my voice in spaces that don't want to hear it. Our voices count. Our voices have meaning. Our voices represent all of who we are and all God has called us to be. We all have a different voice and a different meaning and purpose in life. God has called us to share them with our voices regardless of the opposition and negativity trying to stifle them.

Lyric shared some of her own wisdom with me as we concluded our time together:

> I have a quote I always say that says "we are lyricists of a thousand tongues." It basically means, don't hold back what you have to say because what you have to say may connect with someone. It may even change someone's life.

> Listen to black women. Listen to black girls.

Parable of the
FASS BROWN GIRL

"Who I am shows up in my body.
What I've been through shows up in my body."
—Mary, age sixteen

Mary's curly hair and big brown eyes stand out when she walks into a room. She hads a lot of spunky personality but is also shy in many ways. When I asked Mary what she loves most about herself, she is embarrassed to say what she is thinking, her face turning red.

"I think I'm pretty smart," she reluctantly says.

She decided to come to counseling when her best friend, who also saw me for counseling, told her she should talk to me. Her parents were elated when Mary asked to see a counselor. They are open to receiving all the help they could get in raising their teenaged daughter. Mary is a popular girl at her school, involved with her school's theater program, but she mostly likes to hang out with her friends in her spare time.

According to Mary, "hanging out" is mostly connecting through social media, particularly Instagram and Snapchat.

Only a sophomore in high school, she doesn"t know what she wants to do in the future, but she thinks communications could be a good college major because she loves to talk. Mary excitedly tells me about a road trip she took with her mother during her spring break to visit colleges. The two of them traveled in a rented two-door sedan, staying in motels and eating out of pizza boxes. She'd felt free because she could be a little girl on a trip with her mother. This was the best the two of them had gotten along in a while.

Mary and her mother have the typical tensions teenagers go through with their parents. They argue over what Mary wore to school, about Mary hanging out late hours, and other general miscommunication between them. Mary lives with both her parents, though her mother and father do not get along or sleep in the same room.

She doesn't understand why they don't just separate completely. "They think I'm dumb, like I don't know they aren't together."

Though Mary has a good relationship with both parents, she has a closer one with her mother. Mary says her father is often angry because of how much stress his job causes. He is also very strict with her and her older brother. However, he is harder on Mary because he believes girls need more discipline. Mary is torn between resenting him because of his different standards and appreciating him for protecting her.

Mary entered puberty in the eighth grade, and her developing body drew more attention from both peers and adults. She thinks her outfits contributed to the attention:

> I wore an orange crop top, fishnets, and booty shorts once and posted to social media. Some of mom's side of the family saw and called

her to say I was "fass." They wanted me to cover up. The body I have, I can't hide.

Her peers also started talking about sex more. "Girls wouldn't [allow penetration, but] they would give [oral sex]. That was the cool thing to do. No one thought about anything else." She admitts to flirting with a lot of guys, but she never went beyond that. She overheard her teachers talking about her. "She's just another one of those 'fass' girls," one teacher said. Mary wanted to report her, but she didn't think anything would come of it.

As a sixteen-year-old now, she gets a lot of attention from older men:

When I'm at the train station, it's mainly older men who make weird comments to me. They say that I have a grown woman's body. Or they say that they can't remain focused when they look at my body or that I'm teasing them. I could be covered up and they would still hit on me. The way they look and stare makes me feel uncomfortable.

However, she also thinks she attracts older men because of her maturity. Older men often reach out to Mary on Instagram, sending her private direct messages. Most are friends or random men who request to follow her online ranging from high school teenagers to adults in their thirties. Mary doesn't have an issue with this type of attention from older men because she believes they see her maturity and it isn't always sexually motivated. To her, they are just cool friends. She gives me an example of her friendship with her high school's twenty-nine-year-old security guard. He started reaching out to her on Instagram after a conversation they had in the school's cafeteria one day. Mary says they haven't crossed any lines because he's older and works at her school. She doesn't see a problem with the friendship. Mary has also developed a friendship with her twenty-seven-year-old neighbor. He lives next door in his parents' basement with his girlfriend.

"I go over there to smoke weed with him from time to time," she says frankly. Most of the time, his girlfriend is not there so they are alone. When I express my concern about this, she promises nothing has happened and she's pretty sure he wouldn't try anything. A few weeks later, she tells me he gave her wine to drink.

"My friends were telling me I need to slow down. I know I need to slow down," Mary confesses. Because of this situation with her neighbor, she realizes she's been placing herself in potentially danger-ous situations. She begins focusing more on her grades and spending more time with her friends at school. Mary even gets a job working at a local pizza shop. She loves it, but her forty-six-year-old manager makes her feel uncomfortable. In the beginning, Mary just thought he was a friendly person, but now she says he makes comments that seem out of place. Mary feels powerless against him so she only nervously giggles when they interact. One day, he asks to go to the bathroom with her. After this, she uses her phone to record anything he says something inappropriate to her.

"You're so cute you know that?"

"Are you ticklish?"

"You remind me of my daughter."

"You like the rough stuff, huh?"

"You're such a hard worker; I'm gonna buy you lunch."

"You have a nice body."

She plays the comments for her father who then angrily calls the pizza shop's district manager. Mary's boss loses his job and she's able to keep hers. She feels good that she spoke up about what was happening. However, when other coworkers learn what happened, they blame Mary for getting the manager fired, having thought Mary had sought out the manager's attention on purpose. Mary says she takes these comments with a grain of salt because she gets the same attention whether she wants it or not. She expresses all of the attention she receives for her body is ironic because she has never been in a relationship.

"It's funny," she says. "I have actually never had a boyfriend. 'Cause men are trash." She laughs that sentiment off as she tries to maintain an innocent humor reflective of her youth despite the continued adultification she faces as a sixteen-year-old black girl.

After several conversations, Mary offers these final thoughts on how she has evolved in relating to her body.

"There were times when I did hate my body," she reflects. "But as a woman, I think God sees my body because God created me. I think God is okay with my sexuality. Who I am shows up in my body. What I've been through shows up in my body."

Mary's body is the graceful and enduring reflection of the image of God.

> *A black woman's body was never hers alone.*
> —Fannie Lou Hamer[41]

The word *fass*, widely used in the black community, describes adolescent girls who engage in sexual activity. It comes from the word "fast" but sounds more like "fass," and suggests the girls are acting too maturely for their young age—i.e., moving too fast. In the article, "#FastTailedGirls: Hashtag Has a Painful History Behind It," Goldie Taylor gives some history and complexities around the term *fass*:

> Fass, you see, is a gender-specific pejorative term meaning a girl is intentionally demonstrating the carnal behaviors reserved for a woman beyond her years. The issue is further exacerbated if a child experiences early signs of puberty and develops physically. Prepubescent girls are not immune. A child, even as young as eight or

nine, can be accused of dressing "provocatively" or "switching" her hips in order to attract the sexual attention of grown men. Fass is nothing more than a synonym for whore.[42]

Though rarely directed at me, I often heard fass associated with other black girls around me growing up. When I asked my mother about it, she said people also widely used when she was growing up in the 1950s and 1960s:

> If you were called fass that meant you were loose. It meant you were sexual and hung out with the guys. People who had children out of wedlock were fass. It was very negative. The person that they called fass usually wasn't fass. They were more nonconformists. They didn't conform to the standards of being a certain way.

Like my mother, I was introduced to the word at a young age, often hearing it associated with girls in school or girls in my community. Being so young, I didn't know much about sexuality, but I knew that *fass* was something that I didn't want to be. I knew that a fass girl behaved a certain way and that she wore inappropriate clothes, but I didn't know what *fass* actually meant. I find it interesting that a word so commonly used within our community was also a word that was assumed and unexplained. I grew up with many girls like Mary. Girls who were labeled as *fass* before they even knew what sex was. Girls labeled as *fass* because of their well-developed bodies at a young age. Girls who had been sexualized by older men (and women). There are many "Marys" in the black community whose bodies have been misconstrued and who have been labeled as having unrestrained and unhealthy sexuality.

REMEMBERING SARAH BAARTMAN

Sarah Baartman was a Khoikhoi woman from South Africa who became enslaved after Dutch colonization. Her black skin, larger buttocks, and other distinct physical features fascinated colonial Europeans. As a result, Baartman was displayed in exhibitions and freak shows in Paris and London. The European press gave her the stage name "Hottentot Venus":

> When ordered to do so, she leaves her cage and parades before the audience who seems fascinated with what they see as her most intriguing feature—her buttocks. Some in the audience are not content to merely look. One eyewitness recounts with horror how Baartman endures poking and prodding, as people try to ascertain for themselves whether her buttocks are real.[43]

Showcased alongside animals, Baartman spent years in a cage, half-naked. Like the animals, Baartman was studied and examined for scientific and medical research purposes. The dehumanization led Baartman to alcoholism and prostitution as a means of additional income. After Baartman died in 1816, her body was dissected and her organs, including her brain and genitals, were placed into jars and put on display in a museum—even in death she continued to be humiliated and exploited. Sarah Baartman's remains were finally returned to South Africa in 2002 where she was buried.

The nineteenth-century enslavement and humiliation of Sarah Baartman's displayed body highlight the stereotype of black women as oversexed and inferior. In her book *Sister Citizen*, Melissa Harris-Perry writes how research around Baartman affected American understandings of race and class, "Black women were seen as physiologically and anatomically different. Their rampant sexuality was easily discerned in their misshapen and exaggerated sexual organs."[44] Black women's body composition differed from their white female counterparts. Their contrasting and abundant body parts had people assuming black women were inherently sexual, which led to their bodies being exploited and objectified.

Sarah Baartman's dehumanization was a tragedy with tremendous implications on black women and girls for generations to come. Scientific "evidence" backed general assumptions that perpetuated false narratives of black women as barbaric and hypersexualized. Baartman's black body was abused to support these narratives; therefore, destructive conclusions were made about her and the general physiology of all black women. By being caged and placed alongside animals, Sarah Baartman was stripped of humanity. If black women's bodies were not seen as human, then black women's bodies must therefore posses no human no value. The silencing of Baartman's voice and the overemphasis on her body reflected how society would do the same regarding all black women and girls for generations to come.

JEZEBEL

The Jezebel image is one of several negative traditional myths black women and girls have had to endure for many generations. Jezebel was a sexually and morally unrestrained woman portrayed as evil in the Bible. Nowadays, the term Jezebel is typically used to describe a hypersexual and immoral woman, and represents sexual sin. Specifically, Jezebel is a sexual stereotype about black women enforced during the institution of slavery. Black women were called Jezebels to justify their rapes. Black women and girls were also encouraged to breed in order to have more enslaved children, or stock. As a result, black women were often pregnant during slavery, which reinforced the stereotype of their sexual wildness. In *Black Sexual Politics: African Americans, Gender, and the New Racism*, Patricia Hill Collins writes, "This representation refined black women's bodies as sites of wild, unrestrained sexuality that could be tamed but never completely subdued."[45] Even after slavery, this sexual stigma continued well into the twentieth and twenty-first centuries.

An example of this Jezebel image can be found in Alice Walker's 1982 novel, *The Color Purple*,[46] which highlights different women's journeys in early twentieth-century rural Georgia. One of those women, Shug Avery, is a blues singer the mistress of the main protagonist's husband. In both the story and commentary on the novel, Shug Avery's character is often likened to Jezebel.[47] Shug is comfortable in her sexual identity and is fluid in her choices of intimate partners. She is also considered arrogant and unholy. Her character embodies the societal imagery and attitude of black women as promiscuous. Nevertheless, Shug also establishes healthy relationships with the women around her, embraces her gift of singing, looks for love, and tries to return to her father's good graces. As the novel progresses, one realizes Shug is not a jezebel at all but instead a human being on a journey for love. Like Shug, many black girls combat a jezebel archetype that will likely follow them from childhood into adulthood no matter how they behave. Black women and girls exist and move in their divinely designed bodies, yet people unjustly label them with a negative erotic stereotype.

COMBATTING STEREOTYPES

I spoke with eighteen-year-old Candace about her experience growing up as a black girl and how she came to embrace and understand her body in spite of combating stereotypes:

> I've always been self-conscious about my body. I never really knew how to be comfortable in that. Fifth grade was when I noticed I had hips and curves and stuff like that. A lot of people assume you know what you're doing when you're dressing yourself. It was difficult for me to find cute clothes to wear that weren't attention seeking. Adults would think I was showing out or trying to sexualize myself. But in all honesty, I just didn't know how to dress to my body type.

The assumed promiscuity imposed on black girls harms them in unnecessary and unjust ways, as black girls are evolving in puberty just like everyone else their age. Young black girls are still growing and learning how to dress for themselves and figuring out what's appropriate for them to wear. This is particularly true for black girls who start puberty much earlier. Their physical development is not an indicator they are sexually advanced. In fact, their physical development at such a young age indicates their innocence needs more protection *because* of their matured bodies. Frustrated, Candace said:

> I wish I had more support trying to figure out my body. There was no conversation about my body, what's appropriate to wear, who I should be dating, etc. These were uncomfortable stages in puberty and I wish someone would have told me.

Because of her maturing physical development, Candace should have been protected from negative labeling and guided in how to manage her emotional and physical well-being as she grew up. This, however, was not her experience, nor that of many black girls. Additionally, they have to battle slut-shaming and other assumptions about their sexuality that do not give them the space they need to evolve in their adolescence. People simply reduce them to sexual beings. Of her own experience, Candace goes on to say:

> I tried to cover my body a lot because something always felt too tight or too loose. I just gave up. I was also afraid of looking like I liked my body. Once you do that, people either hate on you or think you're flaunting your sexuality. I was always very paranoid. After a certain age, you know already how you look as a black girl. You know that people are going to think this about me if I wear this regardless of my grades or who I am.

Over the years, I have seen a national push toward helping girls build their confidence and instilling a healthy body image in them to combat body insecurities in girls. Based on Candace and other girls' experiences, I suspect this is another campaign that, while well-intentioned, has different outcomes for black girls. Black girls like Candace have little room to embrace body positivity. When they do, people think these girls are parading their bodies and sexuality, thus bearing society's centuries-old stigma of their bodies being agents of sexual sin. Mary's earlier narrative exposes the lie that black girls are inherently promiscuous. She is an adolescent girl evolving in her physical, spiritual, and emotional being; however, the Jezebel mislabeling paints black girls like Mary as being fast and loose, erasing their innocence and forcing them to defend their own bodies' existence.

CRITIQUING BLACK GIRLS' BODIES

My friend Audrey has been a dance teacher for her entire professional career. She has worked in diverse environments, such as private and public schools, and universities. Her most recent job is at a predominately white independent school in Washington, DC, where she teaches classes and leads an afterschool dance team. The team has five dancers who are all girls of color. Midway through the first term, the team was preparing to perform at the school's annual pep rally. Audrey decided to record a thirty-second video to introduce the team before their big dance. She sent the video to the athletic director and the vice principal of protocol for final approval.

A day before the performance, Audrey received a note saying there was concern over how the girls were dancing. The vice principal called her into a meeting, saying the administration did not think the dance was appropriate because of how a girl's body looked.

"Her breasts were moving around and it looks bad."

Audrey was upset because she intentionally created an appropri-ate dance and would never allow her girls to be seen as otherwise. Audrey values her students and respects their bodies. She then sched-uled a meeting with the assistant head of school.

"He said the movement on the video warranted a certain type of response and he was worried it would result in catcalling," Audrey told me. "If these were white girls, would the movements warrant catcall-ing, or is it just because the girls are black and their bodies are shaped different and that would warrant the catcalling?"

Audrey told the team they might not be able to show the video before their performance and the girls asked why. She told them the truth, saying some administrators felt there was some inappropriate-ness in the video.

"Well, is it my part?" one girl asked.

She was fifteen years old with dark skin and a shapely figure that made her stand out from the other girls of color on the team. She was also the girl the administrators had singled out. Audrey reluctantly told her that it was, but also said the entire dance was the issue in order to deflect the sole blame away from the girl. Unfortunately, Audrey received a message from the girl later that evening. "She said she didn't want to dance because she felt uncomfortable about her body," Audrey bemoaned, then went on to reflect on why this particular incident made her so angry:

> This was exactly what I didn't want to happen. I don't appreciate how others are talking about this fifteen-year-old black girl's body. Men were looking at and commenting on black female bodies, and a decision was made without a woman of color present or included. I think I [am] most upset because I could identify. I understand what it's like to be developed and a dancer. I started developing boobs when I was nine. When I was in seventh grade, as a dancer, I had to

start being creative with how I put my boobs in my costume. None of my teachers understood. They just brushed me off and told me to figure it out. The situation with my student triggered a lot of my old experiences.

Eventually, the administration approved the video and it played at the pep rally before the girls danced. The students at the school loved it and there was no catcalling. Later, Audrey sent me a copy of the video in question. I saw nothing even remotely concerning.

Not even a few weeks later, something similar happened at the school where I was teaching. As I was walking on to an event, three girls stopped me, saying they had something important to ask me but wanted to do it in private. We walked to a corner where they wouldn't be seen.

"We want to know if you think our dance is suggestive," one said.

They were also on a dance team at the school and preparing to dance for a pep rally. They explained to me that the previous year, they did a similar dance to the current one and some teachers made comments about it. As a result, they felt insecure about their new performance. I asked them to show me the part of the dance they felt would be an issue. They started playing music from their cell phones and proceeded to show me their moves.

"So which part was it?" I asked when they finished. I hadn't seen anything suggestive in their dance.

What I *did* see were three black girls whose naturally curvy bodies had been misconstrued as sexually suggestive.

"This would be different if we were white girls," one of them said to me.

Another added:

We go to dances and we have people look at us. We're just trying to have fun. When we dance, they look at us crazy; but when other

73

people dance, it's normal. It's the same thing with skirts and skirt length. Our bodies are built differently than white girls. They tend to be skinnier and we tend to be thicker. If we wear the same-length skirt, we are called out for it because they look at us as being promiscuous. They walk around here wearing the shortest skirts and no one says anything to them. It's not fair.

Even though the dance was fine from my perspective, I wondered if I should have given them more constructive criticism or if I should have told them to modify the dance to make it more fitting for the traditional context we were in. I remembered those girls' innocence and the risk they were taking to dance fully in and with their own bodies. What should be a fun activity for teenaged black girls was instead a courageous act of resistance. I remembered their bodies, no matter the shape, were not inappropriate but created by God.

ABUSING BLACK GIRLS' BODIES

In 2015, a video of a sixteen-year-old black girl from South Carolina being thrown from her desk by a police officer circulated the internet for several weeks, causing widespread outrage.[48] The dispute between the girl and the police officer arose when a teacher asked the girl to put her cell phone away. In the video, the cop approached the girl, put his arm around her neck, threw her body to the ground, and finally dragged her out the classroom into the hallway. Regardless of the girl's noncompliance, she did not deserve to be assaulted. In the same year, there was a similar incident with police mishandling teenage black girls at a pool party in Texas.[49] A video surfaced of a police officer forcefully pushing a black teenage girl's head and body to the ground. She was wearing nothing but a bikini. Other teenagers at that pool party experienced similar assault. In early 2019, the NAACP Legal Defense and Education Fund, Inc. filed a lawsuit against a New York middle school after a group of black and Latino girls were allegedly strip searched by the school nurse and administration because they were laughing loudly in the hall at school.[50] The lawsuit alleges that the girls had to remove their clothing down to their underwear and were touched over their bodies and inside their bras. The parents were outraged. The school denies the strip search happened, thus dismissing these girls' painful experience and testimony. This incident, along with the others mentioned above, perpetuates the notion black girls' bodies can be abused, reinforcing the message their bodies are not worthy of being protected and inviting a universal, callous, and dangerous attitude toward black girls.

This attitude, as well as black girls' presumed promiscuity, enable their stories of abuse to remain unheard. In her first-person article for *PublicSource*, Britney G. Brinkman shared her thoughts on why black girls are omitted from the national discourse on sexual violence, recounting her experience at Gwen's Girls Equity Summit, which is a summit that focuses on addressing inequities in black girls' experiences:

> These courageous black girls told stories of being groped in hallways, catcalled inside and outside of school and being suspended for not conforming to sexist and racist dress codes. They talked about not being believed or supported when they tell adults about sexual violence. And they know that they are treated differently than their white peers.[51]

Brinkman suggests people overlook stories like these because black girls are rendered invisible or are blamed for their own exploitation. I spoke with a girl who recalled a similar experience of being groped and her ongoing struggle to reconcile why it happened to her.

> I remember an instance where one of my dad's close friends groped me. I was fourteen. It was a Sunday; we were coming from church. We got out the car and everyone was walking. He made a joke and as we were laughing, he then hugged me and all of a sudden, he started groping on my breasts. Even to this day, I'm like am I overreacting?

I was like, did that just happen? Is that what they told me in school about inappropriate touching? I was uncomfortable. It was odd for me because he was one of my favorite uncles. I didn't want him to look like a bad guy. I knew if I said anything about it, I'd be called dramatic. I remember some of the women in my family saying, "You need to stop dressing like that to get the attention of men." Maybe it was my fault? To this day, I'm still confused about it. —Ryan, Age 19

Ryan's story is one of countless stories, with many of them ending tragically, featuring black girls whose bodies have been abused and exploited, particularly by older men. Unfortunately, Ryan understood she lived in a culture where black girls could suffer reproach for abuse committed against them.[52] We don't hear many of these stories because, as Britney Brinkman alludes in the abovementioned article, black girls are invisible, which makes these tragic experiences invisible as well. Blaming black girls for their own victimization allows society to perceive them as less innocent. The less innocent they are, the more they are perceived as adults. When this adultification occurs, black girls and their bodies become vulnerable to abuse, injustice, and judgment.

My frame was not hidden from you, when I was being made
in secret, intricately woven in the depths of the earth.
—Psalm 139:15

A THEOLOGY OF THE BODY FOR BLACK GIRLS

Black women and girls being objectified—whether for their complexion, hair, or bodies—is a constant issue for their entire lives. While a cultural shift can end this objectification, a spiritual shift could be the key needed first. Theology offers interpretations of God and translations of how God is revealed in the world, including God's creation of humankind and what it means to be fully human. In regard to black girls, we need to establish a healthy theology of the body for them in order to assert the goodness of God's intentions in creating their black bodies. This analysis will reveal the valuable significance of our bodies' existence and the connection to our larger purpose and destiny, thereby voiding the constant assault black women and girls have on their persons. Psalm 139:15 is a compelling starting point and a scriptural foundation for establishing a theology of the body for black women and girls.

The entirety of Psalm 139 speaks of the author's confidence in God's intimate knowledge of the author's being. The psalm begins:

> You have searched me, Lord, and you know me. You know when I sit and when I rise; you perceive my thoughts from afar. You discern my going out and my lying down; you are familiar with all my ways. (Psalm 139:1–3)

The environment is uncertain, but the psalmist rests their hope in God's presence. Palms 139:14 reads, "I praise you because I am fearfully and wonderfully made; your works are wonderful, I know that full well," which many women and girls have adopted as their personal mantras. Churches and ministries also use this verse as the theme for their women's and girls' events. The verse resonates so widely because it affirms the physical beauty of God's creation in women. Nevertheless, while Psalm 139:14 is the go-to passage for overall women's empowerment, Psalm 139:15 is a foundational scripture for reclaiming a healthy theology of black girls' bodies.

Created by God

In chapter 2, we analyzed the *imago Dei* as affirming the physical reflection of God in black girls like Leah; Psalm 139:15 affirms God's deliberate creation of black girls' bodies. The author confidently declares God was intentional with the design of their frame and substance. Sometimes, spiritual people put too much focus on the spirit and soul and neglect the worth of the body. God took great care when forming our bodies, creating every part of who we are with love and intention. Black girls need to hear their bodies—exactly as they are made and exactly as they develop—are part of the marvelous work of God. This healthy theology of black girls' bodies proclaims black girls are *imago Dei*, created in the image and likeness of the divine in every version of their bodies.

However, it's difficult for black girls to see this divinity when people assume overt sexuality in them:

> One guy told me my head doesn't match my body, that my head is small and my body is too big. —Thirteen-year-old girl

> I have had to hide my bigger breasts and my larger thighs since I was nine years old. —Fifteen-year-old girl

> All my clothes wind up fitting me tight because of my hips. Clothes are not made for my body type and because of that I get accused of flaunting it. —Sixteen-year-old girl

These girls are unable to express any level of confidence in their bodies because they are insecure with their physical appearance and people accuse them of being hypersexual when they do embrace their bodies. Yet, Psalm 139:15 asserts every bone, fiber, and curve of their bodies are part of a supernatural work of art. This psalm declares the truth these girls need to hear: their hair, skin, and flesh are never hidden from the creator of the universe; therefore, they need not be ashamed.

Inhabited by God

First Corinthians 6:19 says, "Don't you realize that your body is the temple of the Holy Spirit, who lives in you and was given to you by God? You do not belong to yourself." Growing up, I heard this passage many times because adults used it to caution young people, especially girls, to abstain from unmarried sex. They reminded us the Holy Spirit lives inside us; therefore, we should honor God with our bodies. What I find interesting is that the adults always emphasized being modest with our bodies and not on the part of the passage that declared our bodies temples of the Holy Spirit. I wonder what difference it would have made for the twelve-year-old me to hear the message God inhabits my body without it being connected to purity.

God created the bodies of black girls as a marvelous work, and God inhabits the bodies of black girls through the Holy Spirit. God loves black girls so much that the spirit of God chooses to dwell within them, as the Spirit does with us all. I asked a ten-year-old girl what she would think if she heard, "the Spirit of the living God lives in your body," without tacking on a purity message at the end of it.

"That would mean I could do anything," she replied.

She inhabits God's spirit, and no one needs to police her sexuality for this to be true. She can navigate the world with her body however she chooses, all with the knowledge the Holy Spirit dwells within her.

Called by God

Psalm 139:16 says, "Your eyes saw my unformed body; all the days ordained for me were written in your book before one of them came to be," expressing how God has been immersed in our lives from the beginning. God was deeply involved in the sculpting of our bodies and equally involved in each chapter of our story. A healthy theology of the body for black girls takes into account both the presence and purpose of her body. God formed our bodies with intention and determined how our bodies would move about the earth. God destined black girls and their bodies for greatness; God did not limit them for sexual use only. When God gave Jesus a human body, God had a specific purpose for it, and Jesus acknowledges this when he says, "a body you have prepared for me" (Hebrews 10:5). Many of us understand why God created a human body for Jesus, but we rarely ask, "Why did God prepare a human body for me?" God created our bodies so we may live out God's will for our lives. Because black girls only hear negative messages about their bodies, many do not associate their bodies as vessels to carry out God's purpose.

> *My smile is my favorite part of my body.*
> *I think a smile can make your whole body.*
> —Serena Williams[53]

Lamentably, a majority of black girls cannot escape the objectification and hypersexualization of their bodies. Even at young ages, people scrutinize their bodies no matter how innocently they move in the world. This unfortunate reality has continued throughout generations, dating back to the colonization and enslavement of the African continent. Racial and ethnic stereotypes associated with black women, such as "fass girl" and Jezebel, continually dog and victimize black girls with shapely bodies. Despite advocates insisting black girls need the same space to be kids that other girls receive, society adamantly objectifies, critiques, and blames them for their actions and those of the adults around them.

Black women have been plagued by the imposed narrative of a seductive, promiscuous tempter, which is how Mary and other Marys long before and after her become "fass." But these narratives and stereotypes aren't true. The truth is black girls' bodies were created by the Almighty God. Their frames were not hidden from God when God formed them in the deepest parts of the earth. Black girls' bodies are the temple of the Holy Spirit who lives in them. Their uninformed bodies were seen, and their days were written in God's book even before they physically came into being. This is the theology of the body for black girls like Mary.

"God sees my body" was one of the many enlightened statements Mary said during in our time together. For most of my own adolescence, I don't think I ever knew God saw my body. That was not a message I had ever received. I spent so much time hating and questioning my body that I essentially forgot God had created it too. I knew God loved me. I knew God wanted my heart, mind, and soul, but I mistakenly thought God's love for me ended there. Any time my body was mentioned in a spiritual context, it was connected to sexual sin, giving even that an inadvertent negative connotation. Then one day, I sat with a sixteen-year-old named Mary and she reminded me that God sees me my body as divine, no matter how society has devalued it. God sees my body because God created it, the Holy Spirit inhabits my body and my purpose and calling are to be lived out within it. Who I am is not a myth or a stereotype. Who I am is not merely an amorphous spirit and soul. As Mary said, "who I am shows up in my body." May I endeavor to live this fact in my daily life.

Parable of the
ALIENATED BROWN GIRL

"I am neither African or African American.
I am a black girl in America."
Nimi, age seventeen

I am Nigerian, girl, get it right," she jokes playfully after I mistakenly call her Ghanaian.

Nimi and her Ghanaian friends tease each other about which is the best African country, though they are all very proud to be from West Africa.

"Nigerians make fun of me 'cause I don't speak the language. They always ask me 'why do you talk white?'"

"How do you respond?" I ask.

"I just don't say anything."

Nimi's parents are both from Nigeria, although Nimi grew up without her father. He was deported when her mother was pregnant with Nimi. Because of this, her mother's family begged her mother to get an abortion. Her mother, already certain of the baby's name even in the pregnancy's early weeks, adamantly refused to abort Nimi. Nimi's mother was alone but at peace in the hospital when she gave birth, certain God had called her to have the child. Nimi's father never returned.

"I spoke to him one time when I was four or five," Nimi says. "Don't remember much after that."

Nimi has two older brothers who were both born in Nigeria. Her mother struggled to raise three kids alone. For the first seven years of her life, Nimi's family lived in a studio apartment. Nimi recalls only having one mattress, which she and her brothers crowded on to sleep while their mother slept on the floor. During that time, her mother started a catering business specializing in Nigerian cuisine. Once the business started growing, the family moved into a better apartment.

"Nobody can resist that jollof rice," Nimi says, giving me her take on why her mother's business took off.

Although she clearly loves her mother, Nimi acknowledges a disconnect between the two of them now that Nimi is seventeen years old. They don't talk often and when they do, they argue. Nimi says they have never had a heart-to-heart conversations; her mother only lectures her, saying things like, "You know you can get pregnant, right? Don't do it."

"It's sexist," Nimi asserts. "My brothers never had to deal with any of this."

Nimi laments her mother just does not understand her. Her mother generally distrusts Americans; and the more Americanized Nimi becomes, the more friction arises between them.

"One of my mom's sisters called my mom and accused her of having white children," Nimi recalls.

Her mother's friends also shame the children because they don't know the Nigerian language of Yoruba. Her mother tries her hardest to defend the children, though. Nimi says that her mother struggles with feeling that her children are not identifiably Nigerian with the exception of their last name. The boys have long lost their accent, and Nimi has never had a Nigerian accent or other obvious identifiers other than her name. Nimi has never even been to Nigeria; nevertheless, she proudly identifies as African.

"I try to do my best to keep that part of me alive, but sometimes, when my mom is talking about my homeland I feel like she's speaking about a foreign nation. I feel more American than I feel African. I try my hardest to rep Nigeria, but then, in reality, it's something different. I feel bad about that because I just never had [access to] the culture like my parents did."

Even though she doesn't connect with Nigeria as her mother does, Nimi has difficulty connecting to what it means to be black in America too.

"I can't even begin to tell you how African Americans used to treat us in public school," she recalls. "They'd ask me why I didn't perm my hair. They were lighter than us and they would say things like, 'Oh, she look like a roach.'"

The number of times she has to pronounce her last name for her teachers makes her angry. They always found ways to mispronounce it, which made other kids in the class chuckle. Nimi just wanted to sink into her desk every time a new adult had to sound her name out on a class attendance list. Nimi recalls other kids calling her names like "African booty scratcher" and hearing her brothers being called "greasy monkey head."

One story from middle school still hurts her to this day. A boy approached a group of her friends and told them they were all pretty. Then, he pointed to Nimi, took in her strong, Nigerian facial features, and sneered, "Ewwww, what are you!" Everybody laughed, including the teacher. She acknowledges she has self-esteem issues because of it to this day.

Nimi says black Americans think African people are less than they are. "And I'm like, we're all black."

At this point in life, even though she is proud of her Nigerian heritage, she neither identifies explicitly with being African or African American. She wasn't raised in a Nigerian home in Africa, nor was she raised in an African American home in the United States. As a freethinking, independent, seventeen-year-old, Nimi now identifies as being a black girl in America, even though she has challenges from choosing this identity.

Like most African parents, Nimi's mother stresses the importance of school. After starting out in public schools, Nimi's mother enrolled her into a private boarding school when she received a scholarship. A naturally intelligent girl, Nimi excels in all subjects, especially math and science. Outside of the classroom, she deals with microaggressions like any other black girl. During her first year at the boarding school, her white roommate told other students Nimi didn't wash her hair because she had braids. People would stay away from her, thinking she was dirty because she didn't wash her hair.

"Last month a girl petted my hair," she laughs.

It seems no matter where she goes, she doesn't fit in black spaces or white spaces. Nimi feels like she has no identity.

"I remember when I was about fourteen, it got so bad at one point I just prayed, 'God, please let me wake up from this nightmare,' and that God would make me white because people made me feel like trash."

During her freshman year at the boarding school, Nimi brought a Bible to school, though she acknowledges it had been there for emergency purposes only. Nimi isn't sure if she believes in God on her own or if she goes through the motions because she'd been taught to do so.

Her mother, on the other hand, is a devout Christian.

Nimi laughs and rolls her eyes. "Can't have a conversation with shawty without her bringing up Jesus." Most of her friends don't know the extent of Nimi's religious upbringing. "My mom initially went into labor with me at church. That's how much it's in me. I grew up there."

She doesn't have fond memories of the church environment, however. She thinks the church parishioners were judgmental and did things in Jesus's name that weren't right to her.

"With my mom being a single parent, they made her feel bad. We were poor and they didn't do anything to help us out."

For Nimi, God isn't tied to her identity; instead, God is tied to her bad experiences in church and what she has learned through slavery's painful history. She can't separate the two.

"It's hard for me to find salvation in the midst of all of the pain," she says. "I have to learn to associate God with God and not with people. But, I have more faith now than I did before. It's the faith I want to practice because in it I think I can discover more about who I am."

I'm awfully bitter these days because my parents were slaves.
—Nina Simone[54]

My earliest memories of visiting museums are from class trips with my schools where I watched my classmates excitedly learn about their history through old photos, paintings, and ancient artifacts. As a child, I always felt left out and thought the trips were pointless for me, the only black girl, amid a class of kids whose families could trace their immigrant history through old documents.

"Look!" I recall one kid screaming to me as we looked up last names on the walls at Ellis Island. He saw my last name on the top and was excited to make the correlation between the Adams he saw there and who he assumed were my ancestors. I amused him by pretending to be excited, but I knew those people weren't related to me. As a fifth grader, the only thing I knew for sure was that my family's last name came from whoever our slave owner was. An unlikelier reason was the original African surname was difficult to pronounce and Adams was an "easier" name to say. Regardless, that was not my family on that wall.

Because I have been blessed in receiving a quality education, I have been able to study and research African and African American history. I have also taken a DNA test and learned how much West African ancestry I have. I've had conversations with older family members and have heard stories that go back as far as their memory serves them. Yet walking through the Smithsonian National Museum of African American History and Culture (NMAAHC) was quite an over-whelming and cumulative experience. I absorbed my people's history in ways I'd never imagined. The stories on the walls, in the photos, in the ancient artifacts, in the videos, and so on are now etched in the minds of every single person who walked through those museum doors.

I have difficulty explaining the emotions I felt as an adult woman walking through the NMAAHC. I felt a range of emotions as I perused each exhibit slowly and intently. I was grateful for the opportunity to experience this. I was proud to be a part of the legacy of resilience. I was sad because this experience was such a long time in coming. I was angry about feeling stripped of my own history until now. I felt guilty as I recalled growing up resenting any African connection to my own identity.

My dark skin, oval eyes, and high cheekbones often had people asking what country I was from. I'd angrily respond I was from "here," meaning the United States. I would say my parents were from the South, but I hadn't known then my ancestors had been enslaved

Africans sent to work in the Carolinas. Most of all, I resented any connections with my African identity because of the negative stereotypes created about Africans, such as their features,[55] dialects, and how many countries in Africa are portrayed as impoverished. I was proud to be black but not proud to be African. As I have gotten older, I have evolved in my knowledge and appreciation of the African part of my identity. Black women and girls struggle with their identity on many fronts, and the struggle to reconcile our African, American, and black identities is a significant part of that tension. Nimi is a first-generation child of a West African family, and her identity as an African has been confused with her identity as an American. Though my ancestry lies in West African roots, my identity as an African has been stolen, on the one hand, and denied in the other, in my identity as an American. And yet this country's contentious treatment of black people constantly attacks our Americanness regardless.

A TALE OF TWO IDENTITIES

I interviewed two twenty-one-year-old young women to gain perspectives into the strains and differences between black/African American and African identities. I asked both young women similar questions in order to gauge their various impressions and backgrounds. Abina is a college student majoring in engineering. Abina was born in Ghana, West Africa, and her family moved to the United States when she was seven years old. Kia is a college student majoring in communications. She was born and raised in New Jersey. She is unaware of any family heritage beyond the United States.

Abina

Q: Describe your upbringing.

Abina: My family moved to this country for better education, so our value is in how our grades are. All their hopes and dreams were about us in college. I know now that my worth is not in my GPA, but that was not the case growing up. Everything my little brother and I did was secondary to our GPA. I remember being really good at tennis and then in high school, my parents told me to drop it. There was no such thing as juggling a bunch of extracurriculars like American kids.

Q: How would you describe your home life?

Abina: We are a very close family because we are all we have had outside of a few Ghanaian friends. This is mainly because we don't have a lot of family here so we have a lot of family friends that we sort of made cousins. Most of the family we have is in Ghana or other parts of Europe. Of course, I know English; but at home, my parents speak Twi to us. My brother and I reply in English. Sometimes I answer in Twi because I always felt like I should practice. We don't eat the same food as African American families. We eat a lot of rice and stew. A lot of Fufu. A lot of starchy stuff. Not the same food we ate in school. Thanksgiving food around the holidays was always different. But my brother and I felt since we were in the [United] States and celebrating the same holidays, we told our mom she needed to start making turkey for Thanksgiving. Even still, it was always different. But overall, we stayed tight knit. There was a little tension between me and my parents growing up my teenage years because of the differences they started to see in me. My mom would say, "You think that you're one of those black girls at school." She didn't like the way I dressed and thought I was too loud or talking back. She would say, "Remember who you are. You are not like them."

Q: How do you feel being a first-generation African in America? Do you feel more African or African American?

Abina: I have always felt American, but I knew I wasn't African American. I have always known I was Ghanaian; but before I went to Ghana, I did not feel Ghanaian. I was diaspora who never grew up in Ghana and I was diaspora who was not African American. It's a strange in-between place. I felt Ghanaian based off knowing my culture, food, and language. I forced trying to learn Twi and forced trying to learn more about my culture. My parents have always made a clear distinction that I am not African American. They considered African Americans lazy, complainers, not hard working, jealous, etc. So, in my mind, I couldn't be. A lot of my other first- or second-generation African friends feel like there's no space for them and they have to create it. But now, having been to Ghana, I feel like I got that last piece of the puzzle. I had been to Ghana and I am fully Ghanaian. After I came back, I was like, "Finally!"

Q: Do you feel like you have any African American identity?

Abina: I take on the identity of African American when I'm not around people that know me in depth. I don't have an accent; I enjoy black American culture and other things so I can blend easily. I feel black in public spaces because I know people are seeing me [as] black. If I stole something from a store or something, no one is going to say, "Oh, that Ghanaian girl." But when it came to the actual experiences of African Americans, I knew I couldn't connect. I came around the age of seven, so I grew up with the same pop culture, sports, and arts, etc. I picked up on the lingo, etc. I only feel excluded when people talked about origin. I don't have family in the South or anything like that.

Q: Did you feel different growing up? Or did you feel "othered?" What have been some of your greatest struggles growing up as an African girl?

Abina: I wasn't as confident as the black girls. I felt separated from other black girls. They were so free and open to wearing different types of outfits. They dated differently. I felt like African American girls pushed the envelope and could be more free. I think it's because people expect them to be that way anyway so they gave themselves permission to be open. They expect them to be loud and out there. I tried so hard to be demure, quiet, and respectful. I would question if I was allowed to be open minded or opinionated. I was angry and sad and depressed because I didn't feel enough.

Q: Was there a difference between you, your African friends, and the other African American girls (and other students) in your schools?

Abina: I grew up in a very diverse school so there were a lot of black kids in my classes and there was a clear difference between those girls of the diaspora that were raised by African families and the black girls of the diaspora of the 1400s.[56] African kids were fearful of embarrassing their parents. We were fearful of authority. It's respect, but it stems more from fear. Overall, we mixed in with the other black kids. We knew we could be friends and hang out but we couldn't be "like" them. We all started mingling together [the African kids and African American kids], but eventually, we started to be separated based on academic rigor and then I was mostly in classes with my other African friends.

Q: How did your African friends feel about African Americans in general?

Abina: Many of them started out thinking like our parents. People don't understand black girls. They thought, "Why do they dress that way? Why do they act that way?" This was mainly with the girls because that was who I hung with. I hated hearing that because I completely understand, because I am treated like a black girl. We are way more like them than we are not. People assumed I was a nuisance or hostile. I don't remember a time I was out and people wouldn't treat me different until they realized that I wasn't the stereotype that they had in their head. There is no difference in how we are treated just because we are Ghanaian. The perspective by Africans that

African Americans are lost in their ways because they don't know where they are from is a myth. Africans can be classist and there is no distinction here. We are black. When my little brother got pulled over by a police officer, he thought he was going to die. I remember hearing the fear in his voice. I think sometimes it's a culture shock for Africans because they realize once you are outside your house no one is looking at you different the way you look at yourself different. In America, our experiences as Africans are no different until we get home.

Q: What role has faith played in your upbringing and your identity?

Abina: My family is very religious. I grew up going to an African American church, which had a lot to do with my appreciation for African American culture, but I was so confused about God for a long time. Growing up, you hear a lot of different black perspectives about Christianity. I know that Christianity was brought to Africans and that it's not our primary religion. So I always questioned if Christianity was forced on Africans. And if so, what is my real spirituality before colonialism? Christians have a demonizing view of every other religion that is not Christian. There is something so powerful about African spirituality. Colonization made us view our spirituality as evil. I want to look into that more. Now I realize there is something deeper there because our history was discarded and blown away. But, I never felt the need to discard my Christian faith because of what I'm learning. People don't realize there is power in pushing everything together. What's the scripture? "All things work together for the good of those who love God and are called according to his purpose."[57] I am able to see the positives in what I have learned through my faith and how I've come to worship. As of late, I'm just focused on my personal relationship with God.

Kia

Q: Describe your upbringing.

Kia: I come from an upper-middle-class African American family. My mom is from North Carolina and my dad is from South Carolina. Eventually, both families wound up in New York somehow. I have an older brother and older sister. We are all very close and both my mom's and dad's sides of the family are large; therefore, we have very large holidays and family gatherings. We used to always gather at my great-grand-mother's house in North Carolina, which we refer to as the "family home." We don't anymore now that everyone is older and the elders have passed on. My family is loud. [*She laughs.*] It doesn't matter if we're sitting and talking right next to each other. We are also a family of cooks. Everyone cooks—the men and women. A lot of recipes have been in the family for genera-tions. As far as my immediate family is concerned, my parents had high expectations of excellence for me and my siblings, but they weren't strict. I participated in a lot of activities: piano, flute, guitar; I played tennis, [and participated in] swimming and dance. My sister and brother played sports and instru-ments. We were always very active. And I practically grew up in church. Church was my main extracurricular activity for the most part.

Q: Do you feel more African or American?

Kia: I feel more black, which means I find myself in the mid-dle. African Americans have our own culture. It's not African or American. It's our own thing. I don't eat Fufu or nothing. We created our own culture. I haven't really thought about what it means to be black, though. I don't know why. I guess it means to be a part of a generation of resilience. We literally created a race. But, I always knew we were from Africa. I learned about it a little bit in school. Most of my life, I went to white schools. I got the gist of it, but most of it came from visits to museums.

Q: Do you feel any connection to your African roots?

Kia: I recently visited the African American history museum [NMAAHC]. It was so moving. You could feel the emotion walking through the entire place. The entire time I was there, I felt [the] energy that connected me to my culture that started with the slave trade and brought you the present. It was almost as if I had been there.

Q: Are you interested in exploring more of your African ancestry?

Kia: As of right now I don't have an interest. I think as I get older, I'll appreciate it more.

Q: Do you have any African friends? What have been your interactions with Africans in your schools?

Kia: It was different in high school than it's been in college. In high school, I had classmates that were first-generation Africans. I didn't think of them any different. I always thought they were just black like me. I went to a white school, so everybody was black. The more of us the better. When I got to college, people began to express their African identity more. I noticed it more with the clubs and the Africans hanging out with each other and going to parties together.

That was where I learned about the African American vs. African culture. It's like we're pitted against one another. Africans think African Americans don't know about African culture and that we're ignorant. Africans think African Americans think they're better than them and vice versa. When an African American expresses interest in African culture, it's like you're looked down on if you don't do it right. You almost feel like an imposter if you try and learn. They're very cliquish. A lot of the Africans I know are rude and I feel like I'm invading people's space, so it's not really a thing for me.

Q: Do you think there is a shared struggle black/African American girls deal with differently than African girls?

Kia: African girls seem to have more of a sense of identity. They know where they come from and so there's a strong foundation there, even though it's hard having a confident identity as a black girl in America in general. I didn't have a black girl identity. I grew up in a suburban atmosphere in New Jersey. I went to mostly white private schools all my life. I had balance because of church. My struggle was accepting my struggles and being vocal about it, which didn't happen until I got to college.

Q: What role has faith played in your upbringing and your identity?

Kia: My family was heavily in the church. My parents were a part of church leadership, so I consider myself a church girl. I don't think I would be who I am without having that foundation. The black Church kept me grounded. It was a good starter to my identity as a black person. There was so much black culture in my church, it made up for what I lacked outside of it. That was where I met God. I will never be able to disconnect from that part of myself and my identity. It was basically my home.

Abina and Kia are sisters of the African diaspora who, had they met, would likely see each other as strangers and have to curb their ingrained negative stereotypes of one another. Both are emerging from black girlhood into young adulthood. Both girls, like Nimi, are finding ways to sift through their identities as black, African, African American, and as women in contemporary society. There is a great deal to learn from all three girls' testimonies about the intersections of their experiences and perspectives. Here are a few key takeaways:

- First- and second-generation African girls struggle with identity formation in unique ways from black/African American girls.

- African and African American families prioritize creating community and identity in spite of cultural shifts and changes.

- The intersections of black girls' identities should include an exploration of their African identity.

- Prevailing tensions complicate the relationship between black/African Americans and Africans.
- The girls acknowledge religion has been complicated by misguided human interference; however, they continue to pursue their faith in God in personal ways.

If they were all one part, where would the body be? As it is, there are many parts, but one body.

—1 Corinthians 12:19–20

THE SPIRITUALITY OF HERITAGE AND CULTURAL IDENTITY

In subtle ways, Christian culture discourages many of us from identifying with our heritage and cultural identity because of continual emphasis on certain scriptures in the Bible. Passages like 2 Corinthians 5:17, which speaks of those being in Christ as new creations and old things have passed away, and Philippians 3:20–21, which speaks of our citizenship in heaven and eschews the ungodly who have set their mind on earthly things, among others, have been used to keep people of faith focused on exploring and investing in our identity in Christ. However, people of faith are rarely encouraged to affirm other parts of our identity as significant to God. In some Christian environments, people have accused me of emphasizing my blackness or my womanhood too much, as though highlighting those areas of myself annuls my identity in Christ. On the contrary, those aspects of me accentuate my identity in Christ. We have failed to acknowledge there is room for our full identity when uniting with Christ. Doing this well—embracing our full identities—involves leaving room for exploring our heritages and identities.

Cultural identity and heritage are significant factors in many of the stories in the Bible. In particular, Moses's early journey from an Egyptian-raised Hebrew man to a man called of God is one from which we can garner theological wisdom to encourage black girls in their African and other cultural identities.

Though Moses lived a privileged life as an Egyptian, he was still concerned and engaged enough with his cultural and ethnic identity that he would go out and see the burdens of his fellow Hebrew brothers (Exodus 2:11). No matter where they live or how they've been raised, we must encourage black girls to remember our common cultural origins. A number of modern African American girls have little to no interest in exploring their African identity. Nevertheless, the concerns of our African sisters are the concern of all of us. As stated earlier in my takeaways from Abina and Kia's interviews, the intersections of black girls' identities include an exploration of their African identity. The two identities are not in conflict with one another, but rather an extension of the other. They are companions, not enemies (Exodus 2:13).

In our interview, Kia reflected on what she referred to as African American versus African culture. The phrase suggests there is competition between the two communities. Abina and Kia acknowledged the tension among African Americans and Africans with matter-of-fact attitudes, neither expressing disappointment nor any motivation to resolve the strained relationships, but accepted it as the norm. Nimi, too, confided in me about the harsh ways her African American peers treated her. These examples of antagonism remind me of Moses's question to his Hebrew brothers: why are you striking your companion? In Malcolm X's last speech before his murder, he spoke of the negative attitudes between Africans and African Americans:

> They projected Africa always in a negative light: jungles, savages, cannibals, nothing civilized. Why then naturally it was so negative [that] it was negative to you and me, and you and I began to hate it. We didn't want anybody telling us anything about Africa, much less calling us Africans. In hating Africa and in hating the Africans, we ended up hating ourselves without even realizing it. Because you

can't hate the roots of a tree and not hate the tree. You can't hate your origin and not end up hating yourself. You can't hate Africa and not hate yourself.[58]

This sums up a cultural-historical perspective of the tension between Africans and African Americans. Tensions arise due to misconceptions about one another despite us all coming from the same family line. Our African identity connects us to our origins, our ancestry, and our entire global community. Malcolm X's argument that black people hating their African origins and brothers and sisters is the equivalent to hating themselves harkens to when Moses watched, perplexed, as the Hebrew men fought one another. We are striking our companions when we hold negative misconceptions about one another. We must discover how to bring African and African American girls into one common identity and get them to see one another as family. We must help girls like Nimi celebrate all aspects of their identity. This will take not just an intentional inclusion of African and African American history in schools, but also participation from elders in the black community to maintain and pass along our history and cultural heritage to each generation, and as well as insisting on respecting these stories from people of other races and backgrounds. The future needs our traditions and values to pass on in order to preserve history.

The spiritual community also must take part in helping to bridge this gap through religious and biblical truths. We are of the same spirit, body, and African family.[59] There are those born directly on the continent of Africa and those of us born in the African diaspora. Just because one girl may deny her African identity does not make her any less African or a part of the African lineage. Additionally, no one can say because a girl is from the diaspora she is not African. Likewise, those born of the diaspora cannot look down on those directly from Africa.[60] God has a larger plan for African people. We have many parts, some of us in America, Canada, the Caribbean, Europe, Latin America, and many other global spaces. I cannot say I don't need African British or African Caribbean people as much as any other.[61]

The burdens of our African sisters are shared burdens with our African American sisters.[62] Like the body of Christ, black women and girls are part of one cultural and ethnic family. One can't say to the other, "I don't need you," and cultural pressures should not force them to choose.

So, here you are / too foreign for home /
too foreign for here. / Never enough for both.
—Ijeoma Umebinyuo[63]

Just like the majority of black teenage girls, Nimi is trying to discover who she is. Nimi's story is distinctive, however, because she is one of many first-generation African girls juggling what it means to stay connected to her African identity and live as a black person in America. Nimi struggles to feel connected to either part of her identity—some view her as too American while others denigrate her African heritage. In similar ways, Abina reveals how African girls navigate living on one continent yet being culturally and ethnically from another. On the other hand, my conversation with Kia reminded me of my own experiences growing up as an African American child of the diaspora. A part of me resented my African ancestry because of the negative messages I'd received about Africans even from a young age. Like Malcolm X said in his 1965 speech, "You can't hate your origin and not end up hating yourself." Only later in life did I realize my resentments were a form of self-hate.

Kia didn't seem to resent her African ancestry, but she also had no interest in learning more about it. Like most African Americans of the diaspora who have been cut off from their African heritage, black youth like Kia relish in the unique culture African Americans created. While Nimi struggled with her own cultural identity as an African born American, she too, found unique ways to navigate her worlds, choosing to embrace the nuances that come with being a black girl in America. Her identity lies in the fact that she is black in color, American in citizenship, and African in culture.

However, Nimi's experience was complex not only because of her different cultural upbringing, but also because of the way she felt her African American peers ostracized her. Frustrated about the friction between the two cultures, Nimi said, "We're all black." Despite the distinct cultures, most nonblack people only saw skin color and treated Africans and African Americans the same way. Yet Africans and African Americans do have a bond that goes beyond skin color. There is a racial, historical, and spiritual connection between the two. Still, the tension between cultures remains. Nimi seems to have let go of the pressure to identify as wholly one or the other.

"I am neither African or African American. I am a black girl in America."

Like other girls similar to her, she has found a creative and liberating way of moving through the world. Nevertheless, we must find ways to educate our youth and community on the importance of bridging the divide between the African and African American communities as we go forward. As 1 Corinthians 12:12 states, "The human body has many parts, but the many parts make up one whole body." The African diaspora is, in fact, one whole body.

Nimi is now waiting to hear back from the twelve colleges she applied to and is excited about her new journey ahead. She spent a great deal of time researching and visiting different schools before narrowing her choices down to a few small, liberal arts colleges and larger state universities. She did not apply to any historically black colleges and universities (HBCUs). According to Nimi, they do not give enough financial aid. She also does not think her mother would want her to go to an HBCU because her mom doesn't think HBCUs are as elite as predominately white institutions.

"I don't know how much my mom knows about HBCUs. She thinks pretty well of Howard and Spelman. But even if I got into those, I think the financial aspect would probably not make it a reality," she says. Still, she knows going to a predominately white college won't shield her from racism. "Two of the main colleges I want to go to have had national news about racist incidents on their campus," she recalls. "They had protests about it. People were writing the n-word."

Those incidents don't discourage her from going because the school's reputation and her mother's dream of Nimi and her brothers having a better educations remain Nimi's priorities.

One of the many things I admire about Nimi is how much she maintains an optimistic joy even though she wrestles with conflicting identities. She taught me I can gracefully maneuver through life while having unreconciled parts of my own identity. She does not try to hide her identity struggles; she acknowledges them, embraces them, and is open to discovering more about them. Nimi does not allow her internal frustrations to prevent her from moving ahead in life. She does not allow external resistance of negative stereotypes, misogyny, and racism to stop her from pursuing her goals. Rather, Nimi is okay with sitting in the tension, understanding she may never have all the answers and challenges will always arise. She realizes that in spite of these realities, she will continually evolve. She has time to grow into and own her unique identity. She has time to discover God, her specific history, and who she will be.

Parable of the
ANGRY BROWN GIRL

"I protect myself, by myself, for myself."
—Ashley, age thirteen

S till intoxicated from the night before, Ashley's mother picked up
seven-year-old Ashley from school. They drove around the block
several times for about ten minutes until her mother pulled up to
the school again and returned to the area where teachers stood with
students waiting for their parents and guardians to get them.

"I'm here to pick up Ashley," her mother said to Ashley's first-grade
teacher.

Her teacher looked confused. "Ma'am, you picked Ashley up ten
minutes ago."

Ashley's mother was so drunk that she didn't recall picking her
daughter up at all. Concerned, the school administration called the
police, and Ashley's mother was taken away from the school in hand-
cuffs. Ashley watched the entire incident from the backseat of the car.

Ashley is thirteen years old now and has only seen her mother a handful of times since then. She met her dad once at age six when her mother dropped her off to spend the night at his house. Ashley didn't see him again after that. After her mother's arrest, Ashley went to live with her grandmother, who was already raising four of Ashley's cousins. Her grandmother tried her hardest to manage all five kids, but her older age made the task difficult.

Ashley's behavior in school has been a constant issue since the second grade. Her school is on a demerit system, and she has been in danger of expulsion for excess demerits every quarter for the past five years. Charges leveled against Ashley include excessive tardiness, disrespect to teachers, lack of preparation for class, inappropriate behavior, and classroom disruption. Schoolteachers and administrators constantly send letters and emails to Ashley's grandmother like the following:

Ms. Johnson,

Ashley is suspended from school on February 9th, 10th, and 11th, for excessive points, disrespect to staff four times, and disruptive behavior. Ashley currently has 103 demerit points. We sent home a letter and information for you with Ashley today, so please make sure you check with Ashley to make sure you get it. Our principal would like to set up a meeting with all of us either before spring break or the week after. I know you work, so please let me know if there is a specific day/time that would work for you. I have cc'ed her on this e-mail so you have her contact information and can address any further concerns with her directly!

Thank you!

Good evening,

Today was better. Ashley did not curse in class, but she seems to have a big problem with her Math teacher. All of her points are from her: constantly talking, very disruptive, always off task. I'm going up to that class tomorrow to see what's going on.

Also, I want to inform you that today two students came to me separately to tell me Ashley stole a pair of headphones from another student's backpack. Can you talk to her about this? If she took them, have her bring them to my office. Have a good evening.

Thank you.

Ashley's grandmother and I spoke frequently as she sought counsel in how to manage her frustrations with the school. Lately, every time she gets a letter about Ashley, she rolls her eyes and brushes off what she thinks is a patronizing tone from the teachers. She typically ignores the emails unless they have to do with Ashley fighting—behavior that started when she was in the fourth grade. Ashley has gotten into fights in the classroom, cafeteria, hallways, and on the school bus. Ashley has said she liked to fight because that is the only time anybody ever hears her.

"I bet they take me seriously after I slap the shit out of them," she would say to me. "I protect myself, by myself, for myself."

We've known each other for the past two years through an adult cousin of mine who asked me to mentor Ashley and introduced me to her grandmother. The first time I met Ashley, she was sitting in a corner in the lobby at my church with her arms folded. The curls in her hair were struggling to stay slicked back in her bun. She was wearing headphones and she very clearly did not want to be there, but her grandmother often brought her to youth events and activities. When I went over to introduce myself, she barely acknowledged my presence, but she did agree to meet for lunch. Since then, we've had a standard monthly meetup at a local eatery where she catches me up on her life.

"It's about to be three fights on Friday because there's a lot of this," Ashley says to me as we catch up over lunch, motioning with her hands like a mouth talking. "People talk too much. This girl Shanelle wants to fight one of my good friends, Imani. Then Kayla was gassing stuff up; then I was hearing that Micayla was going to jump into the fight. Now me and my friend Iyana are going to have to jump in."

Ashley admits she fights because she constantly deals with bullying and people saying bad things about her and her family. She has a lot of pent-up energy and anger inside.

"The most craziest fight I ever got in to—the girl pulled my hair and I got mad. So, I flipped her over and I started pulling out all her hair!"

Ashley has about three close friends at school, not the groups and cliques of friends most girls her age accumulate. It seems the only time she lights up is when she talks about her best friends.

"The bestest friends you'll ever have is boy best friends. They're not as petty as girls."

She doesn't trust people, particularly girls and women. She thinks her teachers are against her because she is always in trouble. In the fifth grade, her grandmother switched her to a small charter school where the same patterns of detentions and suspension ensued. After one year there, she returned to public school. Ashley promised her grandmother things would get better. For the first few months, her grades improved and she only had demerits for tardiness. That changed when someone started a rumor about her at the school and another boy. Even teachers heard about what supposedly happened between Ashley and the boy in the stairwell.

Disappointed, Ashley doesn't think she will never not need to defend herself. "People tell me to brush it off, or 'sticks and stones,' or 'just pray about it; don't say anything.' It don't work like that. I think I'm going to always have to fight for myself, regardless if people are fighting with me."

The angry black women meme—a neck-rolling, finger-in-your-face, hands-on-hips posturing—is at the center of the public misunderstanding of what it means to be black and female in America.
—Dr. Monique W. Morris[64]

Horrified and embarrassed, a seven-year-old Ashley watched her intoxicated mother get arrested in front of her teachers and peers. This traumatic moment etched itself into her heart and memory, as well as kick-started a cycle of personal challenges and instability. Ashley has never had the relationship and love from her parents that girls her age should have, which forced her to create an emotional shell in which to protect herself. She is angry because her mother and father left her vulnerable and unprotected. She is angry at the world around her for leaving her wounded. Her anger is her shield.

People around Ashley dismiss her as an "angry black girl" and ignore the fact she has every right to feel her rage. They make no attempt to understand her context and perspective. Our society assumes black women and girls are always angry, but it rarely asks why black women and girls feel this anger or acknowledge it may be justified.

STEREOTYPICAL ANGRY BLACK GIRL

A video of Serena Williams pointing her finger at an umpire, obviously angry over a bad call, circulated all over the internet in 2018.[65] Some of the headlines that followed read, "Serena Williams Unleashes Furious Rant as She Loses US Open,"[66] "Serena Williams Goes Ballistic,"[67] and "Serena Williams's US Open Meltdown."[68] The *Herald Sun* in Melbourne, Australia, published a cartoon of the incident that depicted a masculine-looking Williams with a large, angry face; big, pink lips; and balled-up fists as she jumped on her broken tennis racket.[69] Brandi Collins of Color of Change said the cartoon was "indicative of the way in which Serena has been, throughout her career, treated both by media and within US tennis as angry, unhinged, really aggressive."[70] In a similar fashion, cartoonist Ben Garrison depicted an image of Michelle Obama and Melania Trump in a side-by-side comparison.[71] Smiling and standing in a pink dress, Trump's small curves were drawn smoothly whereas Obama stood frowning with a hand on her hip and gold hoop earrings in her ears, her body drawn boxy and muscular. Both cartoons invoked the angry black women stereotype Williams and Obama have had to combat their entire careers. In fact, most black women and girls are likened to this caricature in their lifetimes.

In chapter 3, I wrote about the "black girl with an attitude" stereotype. The angry black girl stereotype is its twin, emerging from the Sapphire Stevens character created in the 1950s radio show *Amos 'n' Andy*.[72] Like Jezebel, Sapphire was a negative caricature depicting black women, portraying them as brash, assertive, loud, emasculating, and quick-tempered. On the show, Sapphire was the wife of another character. She was rude, full of contempt, and directed a great deal of anger toward her husband. Sapphire's behavior reinforced the stereotype that black women like her were incapable of empathy. While Sapphire as a term is seldom used in today's society, the phrase "angry black woman" remains and the fictional Sapphire character has made its way into contemporary television and film. Whether as an irate, gun-toting woman in Tyler Perry's *Diary of a Mad Black Woman* or a black woman leaping across the table to choke another person in any reality television show, the Sapphire image is alive and well in our media. It also infiltrates our political discourse. In June 2008, a FOX commentator Cal Thomas said:

Look at the image of angry black women on television. Politically you have Maxine Waters of California, liberal Democrat. She's always angry every time she gets on television. Cynthia McKinney, another angry black woman. And who are the black women you see on the local news at night in cities all over the country? They're usually angry about something. They've had a son who has been shot in a drive-by shooting. They are angry at Bush. So you don't really have a profile of non-angry black women.[73]

The Sapphire image pervades all parts of American society, spreading assumptions, misjudgment and preconceived notions that follow the majority of black women and girls for all of their lives into classrooms, to sports, politics, pop culture, boardrooms, and many other areas.

Every girl I write about in this book has been accused of being angry at one point in their lives, regardless of their widely varying personalities and experiences. "Angry" followed me from elementary school as a child to staff meetings as an adult. It doesn't matter if a black woman or girl is the First Lady of the United States of America, a world-champion tennis player, or a little black child in a central New Jersey classroom, black women and girls will undoubtedly fall victim to this negative stereotype at some point.

I wrote an email to some members of my student government team for a meeting we were supposed to have. The email was really polite. All of them came to the meeting and said, 'That email was incredibly rude.' All I sent them were instructions for who was supposed to be there. Meanwhile, how they were talking to *me* was rude. Then I had to figure out what I could possibly do in this scenario where I wouldn't be characterized as the stereotypical angry black girl. —Sixteen years old

I have a right to be angry and express emotions. If I am expressing anger, they need to ask me why I'm angry. It's not fair what they put on us. —Sixteen years old

Last month, a girl petted my hair and when I slapped her, she cried and I got in trouble. *Me.* —Fourteen years old

One day, I was getting out of practice and I'd made a lot of mistakes [during that session]. One of my teammates said, "Kelsey, you messed up. I swear it's always you guys." I asked her, "Who is 'you guys?'" and she mumbled under her breath, "Mexicans, I swear." I wanted to cuss her out. I'm not even from Mexico. I felt myself getting ready to play into the stereotype, but I just left. That's how we're kept in the box. We either have to repress how we're feeling or go into the stereotypical box. —Fifteen years old

These are accounts of teenage girls from different states, socioeconomic backgrounds, and family types, yet they all carry the "angry black girl" burden. This is yet another weight that black girls are left having to carry and navigate on their own—they cannot express any form of anger without being boxed in by a negative stereotype. They are seen as angry when they are not, and they are not allowed to be angry when they *are*. I look back on my own life and wish I'd been able to learn how to dismantle the angry black girl stereotype while honoring the emotions I was experiencing. It's not that I wasn't angry sometimes—all human beings are—but most humans didn't have to embody a caricature that mocked that anger, and I needed space to express my justified anger freely. So, too, does Ashley. We cannot mistake the presence of her actual anger with the stereotype. Ashley, like all black women and girls, is a human being engaging her human emotions the best way she knows how amid life's challenges. Her anger is rooted in early trauma and helplessness in growing up with no control over her toxic environment. Ashley's rage is a symptom of her childhood pain.

The angry black girl stereotype does not allow one to see the vulnerable humanity of black women and girls. While Ashley has anger due to her misfortunes at a young age, she feels so much more than that. She is also incredibly sad, but her sadness does not get the attention her anger does. Ashley is expressive and confident, but she's rarely acknowledged for that, either. Her loyalty to her friends and reliability in those relationships are notable, yet those aspects of her also receive no attention. Ashley is a little girl with a good heart; but because her anger is constantly in the foreground, people around her don't think to pull out her goodness. As a result, they default to thinking Ashley is just another one of those angry black girls.

If we only focus on their anger, then that is what we can expect the girls to exhibit. If we focus on their strengths, then other aspects of their personality would emerge. Ashley has other incredible qualities—her curiosity, honesty, and leadership—and these are often overlooked because of her anger.

ANGRY FOR A REASON

I sat with a twelve-year-old girl named Tia who was suspended from school for throwing a laptop. After the incident, Tia's guidance counselor reached out to me, wanting to discuss her concerns about Tia. The counselor also suggested Tia's mother bring her to me so Tia could get extra counseling. Tia's mother was disappointed in her daughter and wanted to figure out a way we could help Tia control such outbursts.

During my first meeting with Tia, we discussed her laptop-throwing actions, but I was particularly interested in what triggered that behavior, which was someone accusing her of cheating in front of the class.

Tia had been studying very hard for a math test in the weeks prior. I recalled her feeling good about her possible grade after taking the test. When her teacher returned the test, Tia scored in the high eightieth percentile.

When one of Tia's classmates saw her score, he said, "You couldn't have gotten that—you cheated!"

Her teacher then echoed the same sentiments, "She did cheat."

Tia was so angry that she went to the front of the room to confront her teacher. Her teacher then said she watched the class take the exam and believed Tia cheated. Tia continued to deny she had. Her teacher told her to go back to her seat. When Tia did, she threw her laptop, thus resulting in the suspension.

"She didn't even believe me!" Tia said angrily to me.

I was angry for her. Being accused of cheating in front of her peers and embarrassed in the process nullified all the hard work she'd put into studying. No one considered the precipitating actions when Tia's teachers and administrators discussed the incident. Everyone focused entirely on Tia's behavior, never once thinking Tia's anger to be justified. No one gave Tia, or her anger, the benefit of the doubt.

Black women and girls have many reasons to be angry, ranging from personal challenges to general societal antagonism, to a history of social injustices. In *Sister Citizen*, Melissa Harris-Perry writes:

> This stereotype does not acknowledge black women's anger as a legitimate reaction to unequal circumstances; it is seen as a pathological, irrational desire to control black men, families, and communities. It can be deployed against African American women who dare to question their circumstances, point out inequities, or ask for help.[74]

Our anger almost always comes from a place of truth, be it resisting racial and gender stereotypes, fighting against criminalization, evading poverty and education inequality, defending hair and skin complexion, or enduring domestic and societal abuse. But the angry black girl/woman myth camouflages these truths. Tia's truth is an unjust accusation that dismissed her intelligence and hard work in a humiliating way. Ashley's truth is the tragedy of her parents' unfortunate negligence. These girls are children who have endured great pain and injustice. What are girls like them supposed to do in the face of these circumstances? Both girls chose to give that pain a home in their anger. And in Ashley's case especially, that has allowed her to erect a barrier to protect her vulnerable self because, in her mind, no one else will protect her and she must fight for herself.

HURTING BLACK GIRLS

I have often heard that anger is a direct indication that hurt has occurred. Other sensitive feelings, such a shame, fear, and guilt are also known to precede anger.

"I was scared more so than angry," Tia explained.

This was a profound and self-aware description of anger as a secondary emotion. Mentalhelp.net, a reputable resource that provides important mental health information on various psychological and social issues, delves into the psychology behind anger by labeling it as "a substitute emotion":

> By this we mean that sometimes people make themselves angry so that they don't have to feel pain. People change their feelings of pain into anger because it feels better to be angry than it does to be in pain. This changing of pain into anger may be done consciously or unconsciously.[75]

The website goes on the cite three other reasons people default to anger over pain:

- Anger provides a distraction from pain
- Anger protects people from painful feelings
- Anger creates feelings of power and superiority as pain often does the opposite

Angry black girls are hurting black girls. Ashley was in pain, and in order to disassociate from that pain, Ashley chose anger. I could not let her anger blind me from her pain. Black girls like Ashley have never been given a safe space for their pain to be centered. Many times, when someone acknowledges their pain, it's so that person can exploit it, thus leading to more pain for them. I would further argue that general bias against and erasure of black girls in society are also reasons for their anger. When I counsel black girls like Ashley, it often takes a while to peel away the layers before I can get to the actual hurt. The rage has served as a shield for so long that to them, revealing their hurt would be letting their guard down. Black girls need to feel free to let that guard down. They need to hear we are neither dismissive nor offended by their anger. Neither is God.

> Be angry, and do not sin.
> —Psalm 4:4

I counseled twenty-three-year-old Briana for about a year. Briana had an associates degree and was working as a medical research assistant. I remember the first time she walked into my office, wearing ripped jeans and a t-shirt. Her hair was pushed back into a bun. Her eyes were red as though she hadn't gotten much sleep, which turned out to be true. When she sat in the chair, I sensed she both wanted to be there because she knew she needed to talk, but also did not want to be there because she did not want to talk.

Briana was angry. She vented to me about the traffic she'd been in on the way to see me. Then she vented about how angry she was about her long work hours. She was angry at her friends for not understanding her long work hours. She was angry about the political climate and expressed anger at the injustices she had to face as a woman of color. She was so angry that it was giving her anxiety and keeping her up at night.

After a few sessions of just being able to vent, I finally realized what was at the core of Briana's anger: she was angry at her mother and father. Her father committed suicide when she was eleven years old and her mother became a single parent to Briana and her little sister. Briana's mother never recovered from the suicide and suffered a minor mental breakdown. Briana was left to care for her sister and her mother. Briana went to school, worked, cooked the meals, and helped her sister with homework. Her mother was on government assistance, helpless, and Briana she resented her for that.

"I hate her," she would say to me. "I will never forgive her."

Briana was stuck. Stuck in thousands of dollars of loan debt, stuck in her job working ungodly hours, stuck in her lease, and stuck still taking care of her mother's bills. Overall, she was stuck in her anger. She knew she needed help working through it, but she hadn't known where to begin, so she came to me for pastoral counseling. There were essential several factors in approaching Briana:

- Briana needed space to be angry.
- Briana needed permission to be angry.
- Briana needed to know God was okay with her anger.
- Briana needed to know God saw her in her anger.
- Finally, Briana needed to know God loved her in her anger and desired to heal and turned her legitimate anger into joy.

Briana's case represented an opportunity to provide a sensitive and intentional pastoral approach to black women and girls dealing with anger. In this instance, a pastoral approach limited to ministers; any person working with, mentoring, providing spiritual guidance, or just wanting to care for and support women and girls in their communities can use it. Because of the weight of the burden black girls carry, they must be given the space and tools to learn how to articulate their pain and grief. Black girls also need to gain clarity about their anger. This includes clarity about the source of that anger, their mind and body's response to anger, and how to constructively and symbolically release the anger. The work has to be both deconstructive and reconstructive, reducing deceptions associated with anger and assessing the emotions and their sources practically in order to heal. Both Briana and Ashley are young black women whose life circumstances provoked their anger. Neither should be approached as if they were simply the angry black woman/girl.

BE ANGRY

In the Bible, Ephesians 4:26 repeats the same advice given in Psalm 4:4: "Be angry and do not sin." The words "be angry" acknowledge that anger is a natural human emotion. Some have interpreted the texts as addressing righteous indignation, an anger that is justified by goodness. However, angry energy can emerge from various areas and circumstances and there are many motivating factors that lead to anger. Regardless of where anger comes from, it can be valid and it can evolve into something unhealthy. The grace that God gives us is the grace to be the human beings that we are, including our unpleasant emotions. We have several biblical examples of God giving space for individuals to express their complicated emotions:

- After losing his loved ones and possessions, Job verbalized his anger toward God.[76]
- Jeremiah prayed to God angrily after his continual obedience to God seemed to yield no results.[77]
- The Psalms often invite us to lament and express our frustrations as the psalmist did in many of their prayers.[78]
- Martha expresses profound disappointment when her brother died after sending for Jesus, who did not arrive on time to heal her sick brother.[79]

Even Jesus uttered the infamous question as he agonizing

pain on the cross, "My God, my God, why have you forsaken me?" (Matthew 27:46). God understands anger is an authentic human emotion and is not afraid of or intimidated by it. God knows us intimately and sees us through our complicated emotions. God does not define us solely by them.

Even though God gives us space to be angry, God also knows the problems unresolved anger can produce. God provides opportunities for repentance and for healing. God wants us to channel and release our anger and pain to him. In Matthew 11:28–30 Jesus says:

> Come to me, all you who are weary and burdened, and I will give you rest. Take my yoke upon you and learn from me, for I am gentle and humble in heart, and you will find rest for your souls.

This is an invitation to begin the process of healing—being open to surrendering all anger and pain over to God. This is an invitation to Christ and an invitation to rest. Come to Jesus, all you black girls who are weary and burdened, and he will give you rest.

WHO WILL BE ANGRY FOR THEM?

"Who Will Cry for the Little Boy?,"[80] a poem by Antwone Fisher, is an emotional response to his challenging childhood spent in foster homes, disconnected from family and enduring loneliness and abuse. In the poem, Fisher repeatedly asks, "Who will cry for the little boy?," suggesting the little boy has been left alone and abandoned with no one to help, cry out for, or empathize with him. The poem speaks to the plight of many abandoned children and begs to ask the same questions for little girls: who will cry for them too? Who will be *angry* for them? We must recognize shared anger and pain was a part of Jesus's ministry. Emmanuel means "God with us." God has taken residence in our pain.

Jesus took on the pain of those around him. Jesus wept *with* Mary and Martha when they lost their brother Lazarus. Jesus wept *for* Jerusalem over the tragedy of their lost opportunity. Jesus demonstrated solidarity with those around them, carrying their emotional pain. He showed us how to walk alongside and empathize with others as they experienced their own pain. Jesus's emotional expression was not limited to tears, either. Jesus was angry too. He was angry at pride, greed, hypocrisy, and other injustices against people. He was angry about things that had been done against God and angry about false representations of God. I have no doubt Jesus is angry for the injustices Ashley has had to endure. I am sure Jesus is angry for her and Jesus cries with her.

A good relationship with God involves holding space for anger. This especially includes righteous indignation—anger at unjustness and abuse. Instead of judging the girls for their anger, God calls us to stand in solidarity with them in righteous anger at the injustices that provoked this anger. I make it a priority to express public anger with girls who have been neglected, exploited, and mistreated. I am angry thousands of black girls go missing around the country and we rarely hear of any of them. I am angry no one believed Tia when she told the truth. I am angry at all Briana had to endure. I am angry Ashley has not had a childhood. Ashley shouldn't have to protect herself, by herself, for herself. That's not her responsibility to do so. It is not any of these girls' responsibility to be angry alone or to protect themselves alone. We need to show them we are angry for them and that God is angry for them, and we will protect them in their anger.

> *I am sick and tired of being sick and tired.*
> —Fannie Lou Hamer[81]

It's not that black women and girls are not angry; it's that black women and girls reject being boxed into a stereotype originated to degrade us. We want our anger taken seriously and not mocked. The angry black girl stereotype feeds into larger society's negative perceptions of black women and girls. Black women and girls are tired of having to simultaneously reject myths associated with the stereotype and carry their own pain alone because the stereotype invalidates any real anger they may have. Black women and girls have specific needs regarding their wounds: they need space to be angry; they need permission to be angry; they need to know God is okay with their anger; and they need to know God sees us in our anger. Having to fight off the angry black girl image affects black women and girls' overall well-being, especially their mental health and their ability to truly heal from their deep-seated issues. Black girls' anger doesn't stun God, particularly when injustice provokes that anger. God loves black girls as they are and gives them the capacity to heal as they are. If only the civic, social, and spiritual communities around black girls would extend the same invitation for healing and wholeness.

Eight months have passed since I last saw Ashley.

"I'm fine now," Ashley said when I asked her how she was doing. "I stopped fighting as much because it became too much. I don't like to have things sitting in my stomach. I like to resolve it right away. I don't want any problems."

An older cousin whom Ashley admired sat down and talked to Ashley about her behavior. Though Ashley and her cousin were two years apart, the talk had a major effect on her. Ashley's cousin told her things would catch up to her in a negative way if she continued fighting. Her cousin, who had similar challenges as Ashley, thought it best to start mentoring her because she didn't want Ashley to make the same mistakes she did.

Ashley says she has to make different decisions for her life in order to be happier. She is now on the honor roll; and even though she still gets in trouble occasionally, she attributes her positive changes to her conversations with her older cousin.

"I still fight, but I won't just fight because I'm mad. I will if you're starting rumors or if you keep coming to my face and talking. But I don't fight like I did back then. Before, I used to fight just to fight."

The last time Ashley saw her mom, she was drunk again. They got into a fight and once her mother starting throwing things around and hitting Ashley, Ashley called her aunt to get her. That was about a year ago. It still hurts her, but she has decided to not let that make her bitter.

Ashley is not a stereotype. Given her circumstances, she has a right to be angry. Her wounds stay exposed to the ongoing drama of family abandonment, and the true source of her anger is her pain. As Ashley matures, she has begun to let her guard down and seek healthier ways to express herself, letting other aspects of her character emerge as a result. As her cousin did with her, Ashley is paying it forward to girls around her who share similar struggles.

"My advice to girls my age is, it can all stop if you make it stop. When you get to a point where you're tired of it, you just stop. It's not worth it," she says.

I don't see an angry black girl when I see Ashley. Ashley is a survivor. Given her tragic circumstances, her anger served as her protector. Now, Ashley is beginning to realize God sees her and is okay with her anger, and she has begun to make space for God. She believes things are getting better because of her own willpower and a little help from God.

"Before everything used to be worse and [now] everything is better," she says. "I don't pray or anything, but I see God's helped me out because . . . everything used to be worse when I was a child and now things are getting better."

Parable of the
WHITE-ACTING
BROWN GIRL

"I don't care what other people think. I am that kid.
You do you and I'm going to do me."
—Ebony, age seventeen

Ebony is a seventeen-year-old self-proclaimed nonconformist. "I don't care what other people think. I am that kid. You do you and I'm going to do me."

An aspiring veterinarian, she often comes by to help walk or take care of my dog, and our conversations range from discussions about her day at school to her vents about her frustrations with friends and boys. Ebony has a unique personal style. She prefers wearing hoodies and leggings as opposed to fitted skirts and crop tops. She hates her natural hair so she wears braids, often changing the colors between blonde, black, and red.

Ebony also has a fraternal twin brother who is autistic. "When my brother was first diagnosed with autism, he stopped talking a bit, but I was able to understand him. Not even my parents could. No one understood how."

Ebony says she not only understands what he's saying, she understands how he feels as someone who is different. Ebony has felt atypical her whole life.

No one in Ebony's family has ever attended or graduated from college; therefore, she is under a lot of pressure to be successful. Her mother had a tough childhood, living in poverty and a broken home with parents who eventually divorced. Her mother moved out of the house at seventeen years old to find her own place, and she remains estranged from her parents. Ebony's father had a more stable family upbringing but went straight into the police academy after high school and met Ebony's mother there. They loved each other as much as they loved their jobs, to the point of getting married in their police uniforms before returning to work.

Ebony constantly worries about her parents when they are in the line of duty. She watches the news often and finds herself worried that something will happen to them.

"My dad has hurt himself. Once he had a bad shoulder injury. My mom was in a bad car accident. She still has pain from the accident."

Ebony's anxiety increased with the negative attention police received over the past few years. Ebony was in the seventh grade when the Black Lives Matter Movement started. Complicating matters more was the fact she lived in a majority-black city and went to a majority-black school.

"All I would hear was 'F— the police!' and I just wanted to hide."

Ebony supports Black Lives Matter and her parents have been vocal about agreeing with the movement's cause, but she also feels that some stories are straightforward acts of injustice and there are other stories that have multiple sides and nuances:

Not all cops are bad. That's hard for me to say out loud because people would jump all over me for saying that. . . . I [was] not a popular
person and I'm still not one to this day. I love the friends I have and I'm
fine with that. But in the definition of popular, I don't come up because
I don't have that many friends and people don't really talk to me.

Ebony says she began getting bullied in middle school because
she was a nerd, a teacher's pet, and she "acted white."

"I had good grades and I talked properly[82] so they would say, 'You
so white. Throw some 'ain'ts' in there.'"

She didn't listen to the current-day hip-hop or rap, which also made
her different. She says she listens to anything she likes from old-school
R&B and hip-hop, to alternative to pop music. Biggie, Tupac, Paramore,
and Ariana Grande were just some of the artists on her playlists. *Harry
Potter* and Marvel films are on constant rotation. Though she is confident about being a nonconformist, Ebony admits it was increasingly
difficult to be so in middle school. She wanted to fit in among the other
black girls, but she just didn't know how.

When she received the opportunity to attend a prestigious prep
school for high school, she marveled at the chance to venture into a
new space. She thought there would be more people like her there,
black girls who were different. Ebony slowly realized they weren't and
in order to fit in, she changed her speech a bit.

"I had to start acting 'more black' than I usually am. By that I
mean, I started using more slang."

She soon discovered the rest of the school culture thought she was
being "too black." The popular kids at the school were mostly white;
the only popular black students were male and athletes. Ebony would
apply to leadership positions but wouldn't be chosen, just like many of
the other black girls at the school. She even received some resistance
from teachers, which she had never experienced before. Things came

to a head at the end of her first year when Ebony's roommate and friend decided against rooming with Ebony for the following year.

Her then-roommate, Caroline, was a first-generation Asian-American girl whose parents came from China. From the first day of school, Ebony and Caroline hit it off. They both enjoyed the same movies and music. Ebony says they were like twins. When it was time to choose roommates for the following year, Ebony was certain she and Caroline would be together. But when Ebony asked Caroline to be her roommate again, Caroline responded, "I absolutely would love to, but my mom would not allow that because she does not like you."

"Why doesn't she like me?" Ebony asked.

"It's because you're black. My mom would rather I have a white or Asian roommate than you."

Ebony did not know how to respond, so she didn't.

She and Caroline are no longer friends. It hurt her so much that three years later, Ebony still struggles to make sense of her feelings about that situation.

"With Caroline, that was the first really big, 'oh, my gosh, I am black.' Coming from an all-black school to a school predominately white, I wasn't expecting this culture shock."

Before then, Ebony felt like a white girl in a black school, and when she transferred to the prep school she couldn't blend in; she was black. After that, she says she was at a point where she didn't know who she was and still doesn't know. Everything up until this point in her life has been about fitting into the world, but now she wants the world to fix itself around *her*:

> I just want to be me. It's like, why is it a big deal to just be me? I'm always too concerned with whether I'm acting too black in one place or too white in another. I [like to say I] don't care what people think; but I mean, let's be honest, there's a part of me that really does.

Even if it makes others uncomfortable, I will love who I am.
Janelle Monáe[83]

Seventeen-year-old Simone hesitantly approached the lectern at school to give her talk to the student body. The lectern nearly overwhelmed her small stature and the microphone amplified her normally quiet voice. Simone had been chosen as one of a handful of seniors to share with their classmates some of the life lessons they learned during high school. After some consideration, Simone decided to share what it felt like to be "too white" in some spaces and "too black" in others.

Simone started her speech talking about being an innocent elementary school girl who didn't notice her classmates' differences. She thought everyone was beautiful and that all things were accepted. As she grew older, things weren't as blissful as students began forming distinct groups.

One day, a group of black girls was sitting together and one of the girls had asked Simone, "Why do you talk like that?"

"Talk like what?" Simone had responded.

"White," the girl had said.

"Back then, I didn't know that I could talk like a color," Simone said to the crowd.

When Simone entered high school, she met new people but experienced a different type of comment. The white students would say she was the "whitest" black person they ever met, meaning that as a compliment. She wondered what would happen if she acted the way they thought black people were supposed to act.

"I loved hip-hop music, but I was also obsessed with One Direction. I was torn between two worlds, not wanting to give up either of them."

Simone's struggle is like Ebony's and so many other black girls attempting to fit in while trying to stay true to who they are. In chapter 5, Nimi's challenges were in her identity as a black girl raised in Nigerian culture in the United States; Ebony and Simone's challenges are in being African American girls torn between white and black cultures. There are a variety of social standards black girls have to maintain in order to be accepted in one environment or another. They are forced to develop an ability to maintain the right amount of whatever dominant culture is present in their social environment. Black girls in majority-white environments are often accused of being too white when around their black peers and "too black" around their white peers. And although Ebony did not grow up in a majority-white environment, she exhibited behavior that differed from her peers' social expectations. Either way, sticking to the cultural social script is emotionally taxing for black girls who want to express their uniqueness but feel pressured to conform.

ACTING WHITE

"Acting white" has historically been a phrase used to put down other black people who are accused of acting in an upper-class, pompous manner. It began as a term typically tied to students' of color academic achievements and has since evolved into a phrase used in communities of color to mock those who display characteristics usually associated with white people.

The phrase is meant to both ridicule and shame, suggest black people have characteristics and interests that belong to a particular social script and only that one. In his article, "Collective Identity and the Burden of 'Acting White' in Black History, Community, and Education,"[84] John Ogbu traces the roots of the phrase. Children of the African diaspora have been challenged with gathering the pieces of a scattered collective identity because of slavery. Ogbu argues during slavery, acting white was a survival tool for black people trying to comply with white expectations. After slavery ended, black people had to master white ways of talking and behaving in order to be considered social equals, even though this mastery seldom brought that equality or respect.

Centuries later, black people continue to walk the fine line of preserving a collective created identity in a society contrived for white propriety. While it is true that some may intentionally assimilate for a variety of reasons, I do not think black children do so willingly. Our children are growing up in environments and adapting as naturally as they know how, only subconsciously aware of a cultural script. In consequence, when they don't fall in line, accusations of acting white arise.

Austin Channing Brown begins her book by sharing a story of when she was seven years old and checking out books at her local library.[85] Upon handing the librarian her library card, the woman asked if the card was really hers. After the third, "Are you sure?," she realized the librarian was questioning if the name on the card was actually hers as "Austin" was not a common name for black people to have. I share a similar predicament with the name Khristi. I don't know many black Khristis even though I know we are out there, and being the only black Khristi, especially with this spelling, while growing up in a white suburban environment, I was accused of "acting white" from a very young age.

Because my name was Khristi and I attended a public school that was 95 percent white, my behavior and my voice were also "white." My dad used to call me "cookie" as an affectionate nickname; but whenever my cousins heard it, some of them would tease me and say I was more like an Oreo—black on the outside but white on the inside. They would call me "valley girl" because of my accent, saying I sounded like

I should be blonde instead of having dark skin and kinky black hair. Being so young, these labels always confused me, and I did not understand what I did to deserve them. I did not know how I was supposed to act, and going in and out of culturally contrasting environments didn't help my disorientation.

CODE SWITCHING

I split my time in my adolescent years between attending a majority-white public school and attending a majority-black church. When I wasn't at school, I was in church, and vice versa. Growing up in these two distinct cultural environments caused me to go in and out of culture shock until I transferred from the public school to attend a very diverse private school. Because of these experiences, I mastered the art of code switching, which is when a person shifts from one linguistic code to another in various social or conversational settings. Code switching helps smaller groups maintain identity and belonging within a larger community. There is considerable conversation among black professionals regarding how to manage code switching in professional environments; however, most young children, particularly black girls, learn how to code switch early as they juggle contrasting cultural environments.

As black girls navigate classroom settings, peer groups, and other social environments, some use code switching as a survival technique. No matter where I went as a young person, I knew I couldn't completely be myself once I left my house. I had to find the right syntax for particular settings and I had to move my body in a manner that would both avoid attention and command respect. I would adapt to whatever was the dominant cultural setting the best way I knew how. By adopting situational code switching, black people attempt to avoid marginalization based on their evident cultural differences:

When I go back home, I can put on my regular slang talk. I can even dress a little more differently. I did that a lot when I was younger but now that I'm older, I really don't care anymore. You really don't learn how to be your authentic self until later. —Seventeen years old

I code switch different with my white friends than black. They always think we're mean so I have to put on my nice face and talk nice. You know how you have that voice when you're on a call with bill collectors. My voice has to be a little higher. They don't understand the way I talk. —Fifteen years old

In reality, code switching does not safeguard from marginalization. My code switching may have masked my differences from time to time, but this became exhausting as an adolescent. Young people who code switch often have a difficult time doing so because as adolescents, they are growing physically, cognitively, and emotionally while they are developing their identity and independence. Adolescence should be an uninterrupted time where this process can happen naturally. Young people who feel they have to maneuver this natural process in addition to learning when to code switch are left with a burdensome task.

TOO BLACK

Ebony vacillated between needing to be "more black" in some environments and being "too black" in others. Like acting white, being black has taken on its own meaning. As described in earlier chapters, being black in America manifests itself in a variety of cultural nuances. Being "more black" or "too black" for Ebony meant reflecting the overall societal perception of black American cultural identity. This is why in her earlier school, Ebony's friends wanted her to include more "ain'ts" in her vocabulary. While it is true that black Americans speak, behave, and navigate through society in a particular way, society has placed negative values on these actions. These stereotypes include opinions that black people are lazy, less intelligent, argumentative, and fiscally irresponsible, to name a few. On the other hand, black people have established a distinct identity and created a new culture grounded in the historical experience of African American people. Nevertheless, society continues to denigrate and devalue this African American identity and culture.

John Ogbu contended emerging black culture was a form of resistance, a rejection of the dominant culture being forced onto black Americans. For Ogbu, even what was perceived as negative aspects were intentional forms of resistance. For example, society often disparages certain speech forms black people created, but Ogbu would argue these speech forms were a conscious resistance to white standard English being imposed on them.[86] Ogbu also suggested that some minorities globally have adopted "an oppositional identity to the cultural practices of their oppressors so as to shield and protect their cultural identity."[87] Essentially, in order to resist conforming to white cultural standards, the black community established distinct cultural practices in order to maintain its own sense of identity apart from white culture. Ogbu rejected the pessimistic view that black people had a culture of poverty and low achievement and shunned the belief that black people had substandard values and character. "Acting white" meant adopting aspects of a culture known for stripping black dignity and identity; therefore, Ogbu concluded black people naturally resisted doing so. While this puts "acting black" into context, it does not remove the negative connotations that come with the phrase.

It is important for black girls to feel connected to black American culture. In most cases, collective identity is a key component of black solidarity. Feeling solidarity with one's own culture gives an individual a sense of belonging and purpose in this world. In a society that often antagonizes the existence of black girls, connection and solidarity are what they need to feel whole.

When I was eleven years old I met Kersa, a girl my same age from my church who lived in an area many considered public housing projects. The area was mostly black with some Hispanic families and the housing was affordable, though people of various income backgrounds lived there. Kersa's community seemed very tightknit. Everyone knew each other. On any given summer day, one could walk through and see kids playing basketball in the park, hanging out on their front steps, or walking to the corner store. I loved my friendship with Kersa because she didn't judge me because of my neighborhood or school. She never accused me of acting white and simply enjoyed me for who I was. I tried to spend as much time with Kersa as possible because I honestly felt "more black" when I was around her. I loved going to her house and being in a community of black people. Not only did I feel "more black," but I also felt more connected to my culture.

Kersa was very unique because she spoke and behaved in a manner distinct to her personality. She listened to whatever music she wanted to and hung out with whatever people she wanted no matter what their differences were. Being friends with someone like me, a black girl from a suburban neighborhood who many accused of being too white, didn't threaten her. Kersa and I remain friends to this day, and my friendship with her has provided an essential missing component to my identity as a black girl in American society—the need to feel I belonged within my black culture in my own particular expression of my black identity.

Do not be conformed.
—Romans 12:2

Social scripts do not allow black girls like Ebony to fully express themselves. Truthfully, girls like Ebony do not have to conform to qualify as a black girl. Nevertheless, Ebony and others must resist social pressures as they continue to evolve their own personal identities.

Even though Ebony does not consider herself religious, there are evident theological themes in her resistance to conform. In Paul's letter to the Roman church, he admonishes the letter's recipients to resist conforming to the world around them: "Do not be conformed to this world, but be transformed by the renewal of your mind, that by testing you may discern what is the will of God, what is good and acceptable and perfect" (12:2). Though Paul was addressing both gentile and Jewish Christians and encouraging them to resist conforming to the rituals and ceremonies of Roman culture, we can relate the text's relevance to black girls in contemporary society. If I were writing this letter to girls like Ebony, it would read, "Dear black girl, do not conform." Conformity limits black girls' ability to truly express themselves. It subdues their identity development process. The verse in Romans 12 warns against changing beliefs or behaviors to fit into the world. In the same manner, black girls should not feel obligated to change in order to fit into the social norms of any group. It is imperative for black girls to have spaces to merely exist without these outside pressures. As we discourage conformity, we can reassure black girls that God created them to be who they are as unique individuals.

One of Shakespeare's most famous protagonists, Hamlet, asks, "To be or not to be, that is the question?"[88] It is an existential query that plays out in our everyday lives, as who we choose to "be" or "not be" seems to change from one moment to the next. "Being," as it is used in Western philosophy, explores Hamlet's question further by asking, "What does it mean for a person to exist?" What does it mean for black girls specifically? Being is more than just existing. Being is accepting who one is regardless society's pressures to conform.

In every space a black girl enters, there is a different set of unspoken rules that demands their conformity. If we are to embolden black girls to embrace their true being, we must affirm their being as the unique, intentional creation of God. Encouraging these girls to embrace their being in spite of the temptations to conform is what theologian Paul Tillich calls *the courage to be*, "One could say that the courage to be is the courage to accept oneself as accepted in spite of being unacceptable."[89] Society tells black girls they are unacceptable as they are, but God's message to black girls is, "you *are* accepted as you are." Pastor Rick Warren writes:

> God prescribed every single detail of your body. He deliberately chose your race, the color of your skin, your hair, and every other feature. He custom-made your body just the way he wanted it. He also determined the natural talents you would possess and the uniqueness of your personality.[90]

God was deliberate when making black girls, even down to the core of their personalities. While the outside influence of culture is inevitable, conforming would be detrimental to the plan God has to do work through their being. I challenge the girls I encounter to be truthful and courageous with themselves about who they really are despite what people and society tell them they should be. I truly believe when they discover the reality of who they really are and that God sees them and accepts them as they are, they will be empowered to decide they are more than enough.

If I didn't define myself for myself, I would be crunched into
other people's fantasies for me and eaten alive.
—Audre Lorde[91]

Given the social pressures of contemporary society, it can be difficult for any one individual to resist conformity. Ebony tries her hardest to remain true to herself despite alternating between "acting white" and "being too black." Other black girls have experienced similar struggles while striving to remain true to themselves instead of being shoved into clichéd boxes.

At very young ages, black girls are developing both emotionally and socially just like all other children. The added strain of managing how "white" or "black" they're behaving can burden their identity formation. It also complicates their racial identity formation, which can be important for girls who want to experience a sense of belonging with their racial group. Consequently, girls adopt code switching to adapt to these different settings the best way they know how. Even as an adult, code switching remains a temptation for me in various informal and professional settings. In spite of the difficulty, I strive to embrace the courage to be myself no matter my environment. Most young black girls are still gaining the emotional maturity to acquire the courage to be; therefore, they need the space to develop in this area away from the pressures to conform and the reminder God created them, sees them, and affirms them for who they are.

Ebony and I sat down recently, and she reflected on the past year.

> Last year, I felt so uncomfortable. I didn't fit in—to the point where I
> wanted to leave. I remember crying to my mom and telling her that
> I didn't fit in and I didn't want to be here anymore. I did not fit in.
> Nobody liked me. That's all changed now.

Ebony decided she no longer wanted to hide or be apologetic about the unique parts of her character and interests. In that, she found a sense of security and friendship with many of the black girls at her school who have their own peculiar traits. She is the co-president of her school's Black Student Association and helps plan meetings, trips, and gatherings for members to hang out among one another.

"The black girls at the school are looked at as being exclusive and cliquish but I don't let that bother me anymore." She finds safety in her group of friends.

Ebony says she is finally comfortable and happy with herself, which is part of the essential lesson that she taught me. I am proud to be a black woman and do not take for granted the sense of belonging that comes with being a part of that community. At the same time, there are still aspects of myself that may not fit with in that particular cultural sphere. Ebony's message to me was not to hide or hold back any of those parts. They may not belong to one group or to another but they belong to me.

Ebony fights to be herself, and like many other girls in this book, continues to press forward in spite of society's challenges to that goal. She still listens to all kinds of music. Fallout Boy, Panic! At the Disco, and Travis Scott are some of her favorites. She's still a fan of Marvel and *Harry Potter* films, "But you'll also see me watch BET!" she jokes.

Even her personal style has changed. She started loc'ing her hair and experimenting with different hair colors. She considers her personal clothing style to be a grunge chic; but overall, she just wants her clothing to be as comfortable as possible. Ebony still wants to be a veterinarian when she's older and is looking forward to growing up and exploring other unique areas about herself.

"If people don't like the way I talk and the way I am, then that's their issue. That's why I will always consider myself unpopular."

Ebony is still unapologetically herself—as God intended for her to be.

Conclusion

*"I do see God in that. Being able to
heal others as I'm healing myself."*
Leah, age nineteen

J esus's parables are what critical race theorists call counter-
storytelling—telling the narratives of people whose experiences
are seldom heard. The counter-stories in this book contradict
unfair characterizations and assumptions typically made about
black girls, allowing these girls to shape their own truths and reject
anything that undermines the authority they have over their own
lives. I wish I could have included every conversation I have had with
a black girl in this book because there are many more stories with
many more cultural and spiritual revelations attached to them. Each
moment I have had with one of these girls has awakened something
in me. Through each of them, I have realized, whether young or old,
we are not alone in our shared struggles and experiences. I also
have learned about unresolved issues related to my own blackness
and womanhood. These conversations reawakened my spirit to the
medley of beauty within the *imago Dei*. I truly felt closer to the spirit
of God in every conversation I had with each girl.

In Matthew 18, Jesus calls a little child over to him and the dis-
ciples, saying, "Truly I tell you, unless you change and become like

little children, you will never enter the kingdom of heaven." Perhaps this is what God is doing with black girls—placing them in our lives to remind us to be as vulnerable, unprejudiced, adaptable, and benevolent as they are. To get closer to God, we must become like them, and we must tend to their needs. We owe black girls our undivided attention. We owe them our unconditional love and understanding. My heart aches for these girls because I was once a young black girl with the same issues as the girls in this book. I hated my hair, my skin, my body. I didn't love or like who I was on the inside or out. Like other black women, my journey toward self-love started in my adolescence and has extended into my adult years. These girls will have to start their own journeys toward unlearning life's falsehoods and distortions of who they are.

Thankfully, God's grace and Wisdom aren't far from any of them. These girls have spoken words of wisdom to me that have left lasting imprints on my heart, especially Leah's comment about her story being an inspiration for her black female peers. As young black girls heal themselves, they are opening the door for others to be healed through their wisdom, truth, and vulnerability. I am nothing but hopeful, particularly when I think about the resilience these girls share, inherited from courageous black women who experienced similar struggles and yet also resisted, persevered, and paved the way to build a better future for us. In *You Can't Keep a Good Woman Down*, author Alice Walker wrote, "We will be ourselves and free, or die in the attempt. Harriet Tubman was not our great-grandmother for nothing."[92] With the fortitude and will of black women spanning across generations, I am confident present and future black girls will continue to flourish. I have faith black girls are "gonna be all right."

ENDNOTES

1   Dr. Lisa Gilbert (@gilbertlisak), "'People resist by . . . telling their story.' @bellhooks quoted above us in video collage @NMAAHC #APeoplesJourney," Twitter, December 1, 2016, 6:48 p.m., https://tinyurl.com/yxt7gmno.

2   Kimberlé Williams Crenshaw, Priscilla Ocen, and Jyoti Nanda, *Black Girls Matter: Pushed Out, Overpoliced and Underprotected* (New York: African American Policy Forum, 2015), 15, https://tinyurl.com/y5avexja.

3   Christie Cozad Neuger, *Counseling Women: A Narrative, Pastoral Approach* (Minneapolis: Fortress Press, 2001), 136.

4   Contessa Louise Cooper, "An Open Letter to My Therapist Who Called Me A 'Strong Black Woman,'" *HuffPost*, August 4, 2017, https://tinyurl.com/y43sja5k.

5   Harris Trudier, *Saints, Sinners, Saviors: Strong Black Women in African American Literature* (New York: Palgrave, 2001), 12.

6   Rebecca Epstein, Jamilia J. Blake, and Thalia González, *Girlhood Interrupted: The Erasure of Black Girls' Childhood* (Washington DC: Georgetown Law Center on Poverty and Inequality, 2017), 1, https://tinyurl.com/y3ahmjoq.

7   Epstein, Blake, and González, *Girlhood Interrupted*, 5.

8   Vanessa Williams, "Maxine Waters and the Burden of the 'Strong Black Woman,'" *Washington Post*, August 24, 2017, https://tinyurl.com/yycbzu98.

9   Nina Simone, "Four Women," (New York: Sony/ATV Music Publishing, 1966), https://tinyurl.com/y6q5wtk3.

10 Thulani Davis, "Nina Simone, 1933–2003," *Village Voice*, April 29, 2003, https://tinyurl.com/yy7afwbd/.

11 Donna Kate Rushin, "The Bridge Poem," in *This Bridge Called My Back: Writings by Radical Women of Color*, eds. Cherríe Moraga and Gloria Anzaldúa (New York: Kitchen Table Press, 1983), xxi–xxii.

12 Bill Moyers, "A Conversation with Maya Angelou," in *Conversations with Maya Angelou*, ed. Jeffrey M. Elliot (Jackson, MS: The University Press of Mississippi, 1989), 22.

13 Malcolm X, "Who Taught You to Hate Yourself?" (eulogy, funeral service for Ronald Stokes, Los Angeles, CA, May 5, 1962), https://tinyurl.com/y5nvtjth.

14 Melissa V. Harris-Perry, *Sister Citizen: Shame, Stereotypes, and Black Women in America* (New Haven: Yale University Press, 2011), 5.

15 Ben L. Martin, "From Negro to Black to African American: The Power of Names and Naming," **Political Science Quarterly** 106, no. 1 (Spring 1991): 83–107, https://doi.org/10.2307/2152175.

16 *A Girl Like Me*, directed by Kiri Davis, 2005, https://tinyurl.com/me4c3gl.

17 Ayana D. Byrd and Lori L. Tharps, *Hair Story: Untangling the Roots of Black Hair in America* (New York: St. Martin's Griffin, 2014), xvii.

18 Daniel L. Migliore, *Faith Seeking Understanding: An Introduction to Christian Theology* (Grand Rapids: Eerdmans, 2004), 140.

19 Migliore, *Faith Seeking Understanding*, 144–45.

20 Migliore, *Faith Seeking Understanding*, 147.

21 William P. Young, *The Shack* (Newbury Park, CA: Windblown Media, 2007), 87.

22 Cathy Lynn Grossman, " 'Shack' Opens Doors, but Critics Call Book 'Scripturally Incorrect,'" USA TODAY, May 28, 2008, https://tinyurl.com/y52ms53o.

23 Heather Clark, "Christians Warn Upcoming 'Shack' Movie Depicting God as Woman Could 'Far Outweigh' Harm of Novel," Christian News, December 20, 2016,

24 Dorothy L. Sayers, *The Mind of the Maker* (New York: HarperSanFrancisco, 1987), 21,25.

25 Harris-Perry, *Sister Citizen*, 32.

26 "Don't Nobody Bring Me No Bad News," featuring Mabel King and Chorus, MP3 audio, track 21 on *The Wiz: Original Motion Picture Soundtrack*, MCA/Mowtown, 1978, https://tinyurl.com/yyjqzodk.

27 Audre Lorde, *The Marvelous Arithmetic of Distance: Poems 1987–1992* (New York: W. W. Norton, 1993), 7.

28 Riya Bhattacharjee and Tamara Palmer, "Black Women Thrown Off Napa Wine Train for Loud Laughter Prompts #LaughingWhileBlack Backlash," NBC Bay Area, August 24, 2015, https://tinyurl.com/y43lltcv.

29 Kenrya Rankin, "How Erica Garner Inspired the #LoudBlackGirls Hashtag," Colorlines, July 15, 2016, https://tinyurl.com/y36tvxxk.

30 Mariah . Trapsoul (@CandisChameleon), "Maybe We Wouldn't Have to Be So Loud If the World Actually Made an Effort to Hear Us #LoudBlackGirls," Twitter, July 15, 2016, 8:25 p.m., https://tinyurl.com/y42ehn6n.

31 E (@ElectusSoul), "Black women will always be too loud for a world that never intended on hearing us #LoudBlackGirls," Twitter, July 15, 2016, 10:44 p.m., https://tinyurl.com/y4g5zsms.

32 Jacqueline B. Koonce, "'Oh, Those Loud Black Girls!': A Phenomenological Study of Black Girls Talking with an Attitude," *Journal of Language & Literacy Education* 8, no. 2 (Fall 2012): 26–46, https://tinyurl.com/y2xv4xe6.

33 *Surviving R. Kelly*, episode 4, "The People vs. R. Kelly," produced by dream hampton, Tamara Simmons, Joel Karlsberg, and Jesse Daniels, aired January 4, 2019, on Lifetime, https://tinyurl.com/y2h3cggn.

34 "Chance the Rapper on Working with R. Kelly and Assault Allegations," interview by Jamilah Lamieux for CassiusLife.com, video, January 6, 2019, https://tinyurl.com/y6zrfsha; *Surviving R. Kelly*, episode 6, "Black Girls Matter," produced by dream hampton, Tamara Simmons, Joel Karlsberg, and Jesse Daniels, aired January 5, 2019, on Lifetime, https://tinyurl.com/y3kgaosk.

35 *Surviving R. Kelly*, episode 6, "Black Girls Matter," produced by dream hampton, Tamara Simmons, Joel Karlsberg, and Jesse Daniels, aired January 5, 2019, on Lifetime, https://tinyurl.com/y3kgaosk.

36 Epstein, Blake, and González, *Girlhood Interrupted*, 12.

37 Neuger, *Counseling Women*, 73.

38 Nancy Lammers Gross, *Women's Voices and the Practice of Preaching* (Grand Rapids: Eerdmans, 2017), 45.

39 Jacqueline Woodson, *Brown Girl Dreaming* (New York: Puffin, 2014), 278.

40 Gross, *Women's Voices*, xvii.

41 Chana Kai Lee, *For Freedom's Sake: The Life of Fannie Lou Hamer* (Urbana: University of Illinois Press, 2000), 9–10.

42 Goldie Taylor, "#FastTailedGirls: Hashtag Has a Painful History Behind It," The Grio, December 3, 2013, https://tinyurl.com/y4zcntfk.

43 Patricia Hill Collins, *Black Sexual Politics: African Americans, Gender, and the New Racism* (New York: Routledge, 2004), 26.

44 Harris-Perry, *Sister Citizen*, 58.

45 Collins, *Black Sexual Politics*, 56.

46 Alice Walker, *The Color Purple* (New York: Harcourt, Brace & Jovanovich, 1982); this novel was adapted into a film starring Whoopi Goldberg and Oprah Winfrey in 1985, and then adapted to a stage musical, which would eventually run on Broadway in 2004.

47 Zakiya A. Brown, "Peering into the Jezebel Archetype in African American Culture and Emancipating Her from Hyper-Sexuality: Within and Beyond James Baldwin's 'Go Tell It on the Mountain' and Alice Walker's 'The Color Purple,'" *Student Publications* (Spring 2015): 332, https://tinyurl.com/yy6hvaox.

48 Glen Luke Flanagan, "Student Arrested during Spring Valley Incident Says She Told Classmates to Video," *The State*, October 29, 2015, https://tinyurl.com/y5c5rkaa; McClatchy, "Video Shows School Resource Officer Forcibly Removing Student from Desk," *The State*, February 7, 2018, https://tinyurl.com/y56rpgtd.

49 Carol Cole-Frowe and Richard Fausset, "Jarring Image of Police's Use of Force at Texas Pool Party," *New York Times*, June 8, 2015, https://tinyurl.com/y6r842mk.

50 Anne Branigin, "Federal Lawsuit Filed Against N.Y. Middle School for Allegedly Strip-Searching 4 Black and Latina Students," The Root, April 30, 2019, https://tinyurl.com/yxkfrhtd.

51 Britney G. Brinkman, "Black Girls Are Left Out of National Debate on Sexual Violence," PublicSource, October 11, 2018, https://tinyurl.com/yyju3lye.

52 See Lyric's story in chapter 3 of this book.

53 Alanna Nuñez, "Serena Williams's Top Five Body Image Quotes," *Shape*, September 10, 2012, https://tinyurl.com/y5v9zmhj.

54 Simone, "Four Women."

55 This disavowal of African features is particularly ironic given the fact those features also the features of black Americans for the most part.

56 The "diaspora of the 1400s" refers to the descendants of enslaved Africans brought to the Americas in the transatlantic slave trade, which began in the late 1400s, though ramped up to a significant scale starting in the early 1500s. Wikipedia Contributors, "Atlantic Slave Trade," Wikipedia, the Free Encyclopedia, July 12, 2019, Note 36, quoting Roger Anstey, *The Atlantic Slave Trade and British Abolition 1760–1810* (London: Macmillan, 1975), 5.

57 Romans 8:28.

58 Malcom X, "Speech at Ford Auditorium," (speech at the First Annual Dignity Projection and Scholarship Awards ceremony, Ford Auditorium, Detroit, MI, February 14, 1965). https://tinyurl.com/y6ze5mxo.

59 "The human body has many parts, but the many parts make up one whole body. So it is with the body of Christ. Some of us are Jews, some are Gentiles, some are slaves, and some are free. But we have all been baptized into one body by one Spirit, and we all share the same Spirit." 1 Corinthians 12:12–13.

60 "Yes, the body has many different parts, not just one part. If the foot says, 'I am not a part of the body because I am not a hand,' that does not make it any less a part of the body. And if the ear says, 'I am not part of the body because I am not an eye,' would that make it any less a part of the body?" 1 Corinthians 12:14–16.

61 "But our bodies have many parts, and God has put each part just where he wants it. How strange a body would be if it had only one part! Yes, there are many parts, but only one body." 1 Corinthians 12:18–20.

62 "If one part suffers, all the parts suffer with it, and if one part is honored, all the parts are glad." 1 Corinthians 12:26.

63 Ijeoma Umebinyuo, *Questions for Ada* (Scotts Valley, CA: CreateSpace, 2016), 175.

64 Monique W. Morris, *Pushout: The Criminalization of Black Girls in Schools* (New York: The New Press, 2016), 59.

65 ESPN (@espn), "'You owe me an apology!' Serena was fired up with the official in the final set of the US Open final," Twitter, September 8, 2018, 6:13 p.m., https://tinyurl.com/y3bhro34.

66 Laila Ijeoma, "Serena Williams Unleashes Furious Rant as She Loses US Open 2018 Final to Naomi Osaka," LailasNews.com, September 9, 2018, https://tinyurl.com/y3dyvpb5.

67 Maxim Staff, "Serena Williams Goes Ballistic Over Umpire Calls, Loses US Open Final," September 9, 2018, https://tinyurl.com/y68s74oc.

68 George Diaz, "Serena Williams's US Open Meltdown Leads to Necessary Conversation about Sexism in Sports," *Orlando Sentinel*, September 10, 2018, https://tinyurl.com/yysy3m6s.

69 B & T Magazine, "News' Herald Sun Forced to Defend "Racist," "Sexist" Cartoon of Serena Williams," *B & T Magazine*, September 11, 2018, https://tinyurl.com/yxllyyfu. In early 2019, the Australian Press Council determined the image wasn't not racist or sexist, BBC News, "Serena Williams: Cartoon Accused of Racism Cleared by Press Watchdog," February 25, 2019, https://tinyurl.com/yxhl5dxy.

70 Ritu Prasad, "Serena Williams and the Trope of the 'Angry Black Woman,'" BBC News, September 11, 2018, https://tinyurl.com/y4gmvbt8.

71 Jennifer Chukwu, "On the Blatant Racism of Garrison's Political Cartoon of Michelle Obama," Black Youth Project, May 19, 2016, https://tinyurl.com/y2mfrrj9.

72 "The Sapphire Caricature," Jim Crow Museum of Racist Memorabilia, accessed July 12, 2019, https://tinyurl.com/y34wvffl.

73 Fox News, "Transcript: 'FOX News Watch,' June 14, 2008," June 16, 2008, https://tinyurl.com/y3vwtj6y.

74 Harris-Perry, *Sister Citizen*, 95.

75 "Psychology of Anger," MentalHealth.net, accessed July 12, 2019, https://tinyurl.com/y6mnzaoz.

76 "What is mankind that you make so much of them, that you give them so much attention, that you examine them every morning and test them every moment? Will you never look away from me, or let me alone even for an instant? If I have sinned, what have I done to you, you who see everything we do? Why have you made me your target?" Job 7:17–20.

77 "You deceived a me, Lord, and I was deceived; you overpowered me and prevailed. I am ridiculed all day long; everyone mocks me." Jeremiah 20:7.

78 "How long, Lord? Will you forget me forever? How long will you hide your face from me? How long must I wrestle with my thoughts and day after day have sorrow in my heart?" Psalm 13:1–2.

79 "When Martha heard that Jesus was coming, she went out to meet him, but Mary stayed at home. 'Lord,' Martha said to Jesus, 'if you had been here, my brother would not have died.'" John 11:20–1.

80 Antwone Fisher, *Who Will Cry for the Little Boy? Poems* (New York: William Morrow, 2002), 1.

81 Fannie Lou Hamer, "Testimony Before the Credentials Committee, Democratic National Convention," (speech, 1964 Democratic National Convention, Atlantic City, NJ, August 22, 1964). https://tinyurl.com/y4euk9ok.

82 The word *properly* is often used to mean "communicating with standard English." Any deviation outside of standard English, including African American English (AAE), is commonly perceived as broken, which has problematically mislabeled people as uneducated or improper.

83 "Q.U.E.E.N.," featuring Erykah Badu, MP3 audio, track 3 on Janelle Monáe, *The Electric Lady*, Wondaland Arts Society and Bad Boy Records, 2013.

84 John Ogbu, "Collective Identity and the Burden of 'Acting White' in Black History, Community, and Education," *The Urban Review* 36, no. 1 (March 2004): 1–35.

85 Austin Channing Brown, *I'm Still Here: Black Dignity in a World Made for Whiteness* (New York: Convergent, 2018).

86 Ogbu, "Collective Identity," 23.

87 Paul C. Mocombe and Carol Tomlin, *The Oppositional Culture Theory* (Lanham, MD: University Press of America, 2010), 6.

88 William Shakespeare, *Hamlet*, 3.1.1, https://tinyurl.com/yyap2c43.

89 Paul Tillich, *The Courage to Be* (New Haven: Yale Nota Bene, 2000), 164.

90 Rick Warren, *The Purpose Driven Life: What on Earth Am I Here For?* (Grand Rapids: Zondervan, 2012), 26.

91 Audre Lorde, *Sister Outsider: Essays and Speeches* (New York: Crossing, 2007), 137.

92 Alice Walker, *You Can't Keep a Good Woman Down* (Orlando: Harvest, 1981), 123.